A HEART THAT KNEW NO BOUNDS

A Heart That Knew No Bounds

The Life and Mission of
Saint Marcellin Champagnat

Seán D. Sammon, FMS

Foreword by John Cardinal O'Connor

ALBA·HOUSE   NEW·YORK

SOCIETY OF ST. PAUL, 2187 VICTORY BLVD., STATEN ISLAND, NEW YORK 10314

ST PAULS

Library of Congress Cataloging-in-Publication Data

Sammon, Seán D., 1947-
  A heart that knew no bounds : the life and mission of Saint Marcellin Champagnat /
Seán D. Sammon.
      p. cm.
  Includes bibliographical references.
  ISBN 0-8189-0834-3
  1. Champagnat, Joseph-Benoit-Marcellin, 1789-1840. 2. Marist
Brothers—France—Biography. 3. Christian saints—France—Biography. I. Title.

BX4700.C545 S26 2000
271'.7—dc21
[B]

                                                               99-049582

Produced and designed in the United States of America by the
Fathers and Brothers of the Society of St. Paul,
2187 Victory Boulevard, Staten Island, New York 10314-6603,
as part of their communications apostolate.

ISBN: 0-8189-0834-3

Printing Information:

Current Printing - first digit	1	2	3	4	5	6	7	8	9	10

Year of Current Printing - first year shown

2000	2001	2002	2003	2004	2005	2006	2007	2008	2009

Table of Contents

Foreword by John Cardinal O'Connor vii

Acknowledgments ix

Introduction xi

Chapter I: In the Beginning 1

Chapter II: The Seminary Years 11

Chapter III: Curate and Young Founder 25

Chapter IV: The Institute Finds Its Footing 41

Chapter V: Continuing Adversity 57

Chapter VI: Growth Continues 69

Chapter VII: A Man and a Saint for All Seasons,
                and for All Times.. 81

Afterword 87

References 95

Vocation information 97

DEDICATION

To John J. Malich, FMS,
through whom I met Marcellin Champagnat
and learned of his life and mission.
Thanks, John, for your love and support
in good and bad times.

Foreword

$\mathcal{I}$ have long admired the apostolic labors of the Marist Brothers of the Schools. In his book, *A Heart That Knew No Bounds: The Life of Saint Marcellin Champagnat*, Marist Brother Sean Sammon presents the man responsible for the foundation of these remarkable Brothers. Despite a busy schedule as a pastor of souls and a lack of material advantages, Father Champagnat organized his "Little Brothers of Mary" with complete confidence in the Blessed Virgin and virtuous love for the young. Brother Sean's book, which introduces us to St. Marcellin's men and their mission, is truly welcome.

✠ John Cardinal O'Connor
Archbishop of New York
October 13, 1999

Acknowledgments

This book is the work of many hands. First, a word of thanks to Marist Brothers Stephen Farrell, Romuald Gibson, and Frederick McMahon. Anyone familiar with Stephen's *Achievement from the Depths*, Rom's thesis on the spirituality of Marcellin Champagnat, *Father Champagnat: the Man and his Spirituality*, and Fred's life of the founder of the Little Brothers of Mary, *Strong Mind, Gentle Heart*, cannot help but notice the influence that all three books had on the writing of this short text. Without their research and clear discourse, the author would have been at a loss as to where to begin. Their work, in addition to Marcellin's letters and *Abrégé des Annales de Frère Avit*, makes up the body of literature on which this popular account of his life is based.

Thanks also to Brother Benito Arbués, Superior General, who first suggested that I write this book and provided the time for me to do so. I'm grateful for his encouragement and generosity.

A number of people served as readers of the text as it progressed. Thanks to Brothers Roberto Clark, Jean-Pierre Cotnoir, Jeff Crowe, Michael de Waas, Fernand Dostie, Michael Flanigan, Pedro Herreros, John McDonnell, Gaston Robert, Allen Sherry, Luis Garcia Sobrado, Vanderlei Soela, Brian Sweeney, and Henri Vignau, as well as Sister Rachel Callahan, CSC, John E. Kerrigan, Jr., Sister Rea McDonnell, SSND, and John and Peggy Perring-Mulligan. If the copy reads well and is clear and to the point, the credit belongs to them. Any errors in judgment or factual misstatements are, of course, the responsibility of the author.

A special word of thanks must go to Marist Brothers Frederick McMahon and Leonard Voegtle. Their careful reading of several drafts of the manuscript and thoughtful advice helped the author correct a number of historical inaccuracies.

A final word of thanks to Sister Marie Kraus, SNDdeN, who edited the text. She is a master at finding a deft phrase and for attacking the 'clutter, clutter, clutter' that fills the work of many writers. Thanks, once again, Marie, for your help.

This account was written with lay men and women in mind, though others may also find it of interest. It is, of course, incomplete and influenced by the author's affection for Marcellin Champagnat. It is not meant to be an historical or biographical record of his life. Several others have taken on those challenges with more satisfying results. A list of their publications appears in the References section at the end of this book. The author hopes, though, that the few stories recorded here will help the reader come to know better Marcellin Champagnat, the remarkable man who founded the Little Brothers of Mary.

The book was a pleasure to write. It was like taking a class with Marcellin: he the teacher, the subject his life, and I the only student. I hope that one day, when I meet him face to face, he will be compassionate in grading the work of this erstwhile student of his. Judging from the evidence that I uncovered in writing the book, I have no doubt that he will.

This book is dedicated to John J. Malich, FMS. I had the good fortune to first meet John in 1961; I was 14, he 25. Through John, I met Marcellin Champagnat and learned of his life and mission. That encounter changed the direction of my life. During the intervening years, John has become a brother and dear friend to me. His love and support, more than he may know, have sustained me in good and bad times. What a blessing. I am very grateful.

Introduction

$\mathcal{D}$ear Reader,

Who was Saint Marcellin Champagnat? We know that he was a pioneer member and priest of the Society of Mary, and the founder of its Little Brothers, recognized worldwide today as the Institute of the Marist Brothers. Yes, he was all these things, but he was also so much more. This book sets out to uncover the message that his life and mission hold for us today.

The story of this young priest takes us back to late eighteenth and early nineteenth-century France. Get ready to walk its roads and to cherish the terrain he so loved, to meet the people who shaped him, to suffer through the adversity that strengthened him, and, in the end, to be seized by the God who was at the center of his life.

Marcellin Champagnat loved young people. They, in turn, found his enthusiasm and energy contagious. Three elements fueled his passion for life and shaped his spirituality: an awareness of God's presence, an unwavering confidence in Mary and her protection, and the two uncomplicated virtues of simplicity and humility.

As a founder Marcellin was young, aged twenty-seven years, when he asked his first two recruits to join him. He gave his Little Brothers a clear mission. Proclaim the Word of God directly to the young, he said, and, among them, to those most neglected.

He knew that to teach young people you had to love them first. Marcellin guided his life and work by that principle, and expected his brothers to do the same.

So, turn the page, and begin to walk alongside this man whom our Church calls a very modern-day saint, an apostle to youth. Marcellin Champagnat was both for his time in history; he is no less for ours today.

Seán D. Sammon, FMS
Rome, Italy
22 January 2000
Feast of Venerable Brother François

Chapter I

In the Beginning

$\mathcal{A}$ war, one man, and three women helped shape him. Marcellin Champagnat, the ninth of ten children, was born in the hamlet of Le Rosey, France on May 20th, 1789. Within a few weeks a revolution was underway in the country. The Bastille, a Paris prison of notorious reputation, fell in mid-July. The freeing of its seven captives, though largely symbolic in nature, hinted to the people of late eighteenth-century France that their world was going to change.

The French Revolution was a time of exuberance and excess. Liberty, equality, and fraternity kept company with those who carted off all but one of the church bells in the town of Marlhes to be cast as cannon. Numbered among the latter and a willing participant was Jean-Baptiste Champagnat, father of the future saint. He was one of the better-off peasant proprietors of the region and a man of some education.

At first, Jean-Baptiste welcomed the revolution, both for its ideals and for what he stood to gain from its success. In time, however, he came to reject its excesses. They were many: the execution of King Louis XVI in 1793; a burdensome conscription policy, initiated by the Paris government to fight revolutionary wars against France's enemies; orders to hunt down priests and fugitive soldiers.

As 1791 came to a close, Jean-Baptiste Champagnat was evidently the most important revolutionary leader in town. By 1793, however, it was apparent that his ardor for the movement had cooled. His cousin Ducros, a man who had signed as a witness at Marcellin's baptism, attempted to reignite Jean-Baptiste's enthusiasm for the spirit of 1789. However, Ducros was among those who used the revolution as a means to improve their lot in life. Unlike Marcellin's father, his cousin profited materially from the many confiscations that came in the revolution's wake. He later fell from power, was imprisoned, and in 1795, was shot while being transferred from one prison to another. His wife had apparently slipped him a knife, with which he killed one policeman; others on the scene shot him before he could kill anyone else. Marcellin, though only six years of age, would, no doubt, have learned some of the details of Ducros's untimely end.

Throughout the revolutionary times, Jean-Baptiste distinguished himself as a man of patience, moderation, and political know-how. During his tenures as Town Clerk, Colonel of the National Guard, Deputy, Magistrate, and President of Municipal Administration, one person, Paul Lardon, was executed at Marlhes. No one else was taken away, the church was neither burned nor sold. As a thinker, revolutionary, government official, tradesman, and farmer, what gifts did Jean-Baptiste pass along to his son? Discernment, compassion for others, diplomacy, a head for business, the skills of a laborer.

What about the women who influenced Marcellin? Marie Thérèse Chirat, his mother, was the first. A prudent person of steadfast character, she married Jean-Baptiste in 1775. Marked by utter integrity, sterling faith, and a love of work, this woman instilled in her son the rudiments of prayer and the first stirring of his vocation.

Louise Champagnat was the second woman to influence Marcellin. A religious Sister of Saint Joseph and a sister to Jean-Baptiste, she sought sanctuary with his family during the days of revolutionary excess. Expelled from her convent by the new government and no lover of the revolutionary movement, she once described it to young Marcellin as something crueler than any beast. Louise assisted in the boy's early religious formation; she was probably the first to model for him the merging of a life of prayer with one of apostolic effort. Among the works of her Sisters of Saint Joseph, education held a place of prominence.

Finally, there was Mary, the mother of Jesus. While a later arrival in Marcellin's life, in the end, she would make all the difference. Devotion to her was part of the rich texture of faith in the local dioceses of Lyons and Le Puy. Marcellin would later place Mary at the center of the community of brothers he would found. In keeping with the spirituality of his times and particularly of the region around Marlhes, she became eventually for him a "Good Mother, his Ordinary Resource."

So, a war, one man, and three women were there at the outset. Taking these facts as our starting point, let's begin to answer this question: Who was Marcellin Champagnat? We know that he was a founding member and priest of the Society of Mary, and the founder of its Little Brothers. We realize, too, that he was a citizen of late eighteenth and early nineteenth-century France, very much a man of his times with all the virtues and limits that such a description implies. But who was he, really? A look at some of the events, elements, and people that shaped his early life will help us to find an answer to that question.

In the beginning

Marcellin Champagnat was baptized within twenty-four hours of his birth, on Ascension Thursday, 1789. He lived his life of fifty-one years book-ended between insurrections: one in 1789, another about forty years later. The intervening period saw successive revolutionary governments, the rule of Napoleon, the Bourbon restoration, the Revolution of 1830, the Orleans monarchy, and the uprising at Lyons in 1834.

Other revolutions were also underway; initially less noticeable perhaps, they were just as sweeping in scope and unsettling in outcome. The Industrial Revolution, for example, got underway after 1830 and transformed the world of work; it brought with it the exploitation of laborers and a radical change in their way of living.

For some, the political and social tremors that swept over Europe during the late eighteenth and early nineteenth centuries came as a surprise. Fissures, however, had been evident in the old terrain for years before the first shock wave hit. Any student of history could have sensed that eventually the pent-up frustration of the people of the period would lead them to throw off the yoke of oppression. "Our rights were unknown," declared Jean-Baptiste Champagnat during an impassioned speech from the public rostrum in Marlhes, "we have discovered them; the new Constitution is written, now we must support it."

Other factors

Terrain also shaped young Marcellin Champagnat. Growing up in a region known as the Massif Central, he knew open fields, quiet rivulets, pine forests. But nature is capricious in that part of France; at times, it can be actually dangerous. From the heights of Mount Pilat in the north, cold winds bring winter frost; often enough, unseasonable snowstorms blanket the region. Excessive rain, borne on strong winds from the south, can also damage the young crops of grain. Where the winters are hard, locals learn how to endure. The terrain of his region taught Marcellin these virtues: tenacity, adaptability, and toughness.

Years later, as a young priest, Marcellin lived about thirty kilometers to the north. There the steep slopes of Mount Pilat, and the region's narrow valleys, rushing waters, and deep snow-drifts worked together to create a treacherous terrain. Zealous for his flock, the curate often took the rough paths that traversed the ridge. On at least one occasion, the journey almost cost him his life.

Marcellin's early education

During the nineteenth century, France's rural villages and hamlets lagged far behind more developed urban centers in opportunities for formal education. More than twenty years of revolution and external wars had also done little to secure the place of teaching and learning in the overall scheme of things. Marlhes, for example, was without a regular school for several years. From time to time, one or another itinerant teacher came to town and offered instruction in reading and writing. However, this service was available only to the children of families willing to pay a fee.

Marcellin attended school for a very brief time. He failed to demonstrate much capacity for academic work; the brutal treatment that teachers meted out to students also worked against his settling in. By age eleven, the young man decided that he preferred farm work to the world of books.

Just why Jean-Baptiste, a man of some education with a library in his home, did not insist that his son receive a solid formal education is perplexing. Be that as it may, when Marcellin set out for the seminary at age sixteen, he took with him his lack of education. This deficiency was to be a cross for him throughout his life.

Call to be a priest

After the revolution, the power of the Catholic Church in France was greatly diminished. Napoleon Bonaparte eventually gave the Church greater freedom but for a specific reason: he planned to use the Church as a prop for his regime.

In 1803, Joseph Fesch, an uncle of Napoleon, was installed as bishop of the Diocese of Lyons. Finding his priests devastated by the ravages of the Revolution, he set out energetically to renew the strength of the clergy. Part of his plan called for new minor seminaries in Verrières and Alix. To fill them with candidates, the new bishop encouraged staff at the major and minor seminaries to devote some of their vacation time to recruiting vocations.

As a result, in 1803 a priest arrived at the presbytery in Marlhes. He asked the pastor to suggest likely candidates for the seminary but met with disappointment. Father Allirot, the parish priest, confessed that he could think of none. After a few moments, however, he revised his assessment and suggested that his visitor might try the Champagnat household.

Among the boys at home that day, Marcellin alone showed any interest when the proposal to train for the priesthood was presented. However, the young man was almost functionally illiterate. While he expressed himself freely in the dialect common around Marlhes, his reading and writing knowledge of French, a necessary prerequisite for the study of Latin and other subjects, was rudimentary at best.

His father, Jean-Baptiste, doubtful about his son's capacity for the years of study necessary for ordination, frequently challenged his intentions. Marcellin, taken with the idea of being a priest, asked to be given a chance to test his suitability.

Preparing for the seminary

When Marcellin decided to study for the priesthood, he set out at last to acquire an education. In this quest, he enlisted the aid of his sister Marie-Anne's husband, Benoît Arnaud. His brother-in-law, once a seminarian, was considered to be a well-educated, well-esteemed, and influential man. He was also a teacher with a recognized school. Marcellin moved to the town of Saint-Sauveur and lived with his sister and her family for some months during the years 1803, 1804, and 1805.

Progress was slow, however, and the young man did not show much promise. Eventually, the teacher advised his charge to forget his studies and to do something else with his life. "Sooner or later," Arnaud counseled, "and the sooner the better, you will give up this idea of yours, and you will regret having caused so much expense, having wasted your time, and perhaps having ruined your health."

The sudden death of Marcellin's father, in 1804, was another blow to the young man. With the frustration of studies, and now the death of his father, surely he must have toyed with the thought of heading for home and helping out on the family farm. That type of work, after all, was in his blood; he loved it. For whatever reason, however, Marcellin decided to persist in pursuing his studies. Perhaps his mother's encouragement kept him going. His first biographer, Brother Jean-Baptiste Furet, tells us that during this "period Marcellin approached the sacraments more frequently, took more time to pray, and recommended his intentions to Mary."

Important formative influence

During his months in Saint-Sauveur, Marcellin had the good fortune to associate with the young priest of the parish, Father Jean-Baptiste Soutrenon. A native of the village, ordained in 1790, he was a friendly and likable man who had suffered greatly at the hands of the Revolution. Father Soutrenon lived poorly and was extraordinarily effective in attending to the needs of his parishioners. Speaking with them in the dialect of the region, for example, he was often known to roll up his sleeves to help them with their farm work.

Soutrenon also got along famously with the children and young people of the parish. Marcellin, in all probability, served many of the young priest's Masses, accompanied him when he visited Marie Thérèse's family (who lived in the area), and absorbed the pastoral and compassionate outlook that Soutrenon showed in his dealings with people. Years later, it was obvious that Marcellin modeled himself as a priest after this fervent and courageous young curate. Father Soutrenon was a great inspiration to the young man, and on his return from Saint-Sauveur, Marcellin was more determined than ever to be a priest.

He would need all the inspiration that he could get. Where Father Soutrenon was encouraging, Marcellin's brother-in-law, Benoît Arnaud, was not. Convinced that the young man lacked the talents necessary for preparation for priesthood, he advised Marcellin's mother against letting him pursue his dream. "Your boy is obstinate in his desire to study," said Arnaud, "but you would be wrong in allowing him to do so; he has too few talents to succeed."

Perhaps a pilgrimage will help

Despite his brother-in-law's pessimistic assessment of his abilities, Marcellin felt more drawn to being a priest than ever before. The thought absorbed him. Sensing her son's preoccupation with his dream, Marie Thérèse suggested a pilgrimage to the shrine of Saint John Francis Regis at La Louvesc. The saint's relics, hidden during the Revolution, had been restored to the shrine, and devotion to him, always strong in the region, had sprung up publicly once again.

John Francis Regis had often said that Marlhes had a sense of God; he loved coming to the place and had visited it three times during his short but fruitful apostolate. With haste, mother and son set out on the three day round trip journey to La Louvesc.

There can be little doubt that Marie Thérèse was determined to do what she could to encourage her son to follow his priestly vocation.

On their return from the pilgrimage, and in spite of his brother-in-law's strong opposition, Marcellin told his family that he planned to enter the minor seminary. He was convinced that that was what God wanted him to do and he was determined to comply.

Reflection questions

Who are the people who have helped you shape your life's dream and encouraged you to live it out? In what specific ways did they help?

What events in your life gave you a sense of God's dream for you? The Lord mapped out a journey for you; what milestones along the road helped you find your way?

Chapter II

The Seminary Years

*F*ather Périer was the mainstay of the minor seminary at Verrières. Like Father Soutrenon, here was another priest who had suffered greatly during the Revolution, coming, on at least one occasion, close to death. Most of his young charges were housed in a large but dilapidated parish house; he found space for the overflow in a nearby barn. By the time Marcellin arrived, the group was made up of somewhere between eighty and one hundred young men.

Conditions at the makeshift seminary were harsh. A student by the name of Duplay, for example, gave this description of life there: "For a dormitory we had a loft under the tiles, reached by a ladder. The ill-fitted windows were covered with paper only; you froze in winter and baked in summer!" The seminarians, fortunately, had youth in their favor and were willing to endure these and other hardships.

Marcellin was older than many of his classmates. While academically unimpressive, he excelled in those tasks that required manual work. Simply put, when offered a physical challenge, he would shine. Throughout his seminary days, the young man had to fight against taking an easy way out and seeking more tangible results by working with his hands.

Those who possessed the practical skills needed to maintain

the seminary undoubtedly found plenty to do. As one historian of the period recounts, "During their free time, the young men worked to improve the house. Rotted floorboards were cut away, and new ones slotted in; cracks and holes in the walls were stoned up and plastered over; paper and, later, glass covered the missing window panes. These mountain boys were used to hard work."

Marcellin's first year ended on an unhappy note. Father Périer concluded that he was unsuited for priesthood. The priest told the young man and his mother that he would not be welcomed back to the seminary for a second year. The decision upset and discouraged Marcellin. Father Granottier who gave evidence for the future saint's beatification tells us, "After a year of fruitless study, the young man wept because it was considered useless to make another attempt." Marie Thérèse, while disappointed, immediately set about to resolve this crisis in her son's life. Her first recourse was to prayer. Julienne Epalle, a neighbor of the Champagnat family, reports: "At the end of Marcellin's first year of study, the Superior of the minor seminary found that the boy had not enough talent to continue. This afflicted Marcellin very much, but his mother restored his courage, saying, 'We will go to La Louvesc.'"

With mother and son's second pilgrimage together to the shrine of Saint John Francis Regis behind them, Marie Thérèse used some very human means to further her son's cause. The parish priest, Father Allirot, was well connected at the seminary, and she prevailed upon him to intervene. She also sought the help of Father Linossier, a well-respected, highly qualified, and newly arrived member of the seminary staff. Due to the combined efforts of these two men, the Superior at Verrières reversed his decision and agreed to readmit Marcellin. The matter was settled.

All not well at the seminary

The seminary suffered from a number of growing pains. It had all the defects of any institution opened without sufficient material resources. Staff morale was low, discipline slack, and the teachers, two priests and five laymen, inexperienced and not of the best quality. Father Bochard, a priest given responsibility for overseeing seminary education, evaluated the situation as follows: "These teachers, Mr. Crepu excepted, have not in general the standard and manner of living that would give evidence of pious and zealous hearts. It seems that several go to Communion only rarely. There is not between them and their superiors sufficient understanding and harmony."

Adding to difficulties at the seminary was its lack of a well-regulated program of studies. This was a serious defect. Many of the students were backward and rather old for a minor seminary. On arrival, they were assigned to classes based on their degree of knowledge. This policy led to a mixing of age groups, hardly an ideal situation. The by now Cardinal Fesch, however, was seemingly unperturbed by the predicament. He advised indulgence on the part of teachers, telling them that it was better to plough the Lord's fields with asses than to have them lie fallow.

Marcellin's problems continue

Marcellin spent eight years at Verrières. Conditions at the seminary gradually improved. Father Périer, founder of the place, was a good-natured soul, but lacked the skills of an administrator and disciplinarian. While the addition to the staff of Father Linossier improved conditions somewhat, it took the arrival of the new superior, Father Barou, in 1809 to begin to turn the place around. Very quickly conditions of life and study improved.

Marcellin's second year in 1806 got off to a better start than his first. While he found himself in a bigger class, his teacher, Mr. Chomarez, tried to improve the discipline and made Latin available to those who wished to study the subject. The youth, in spite of his weakness in grammar, took up the challenge.

Marcellin, who by this time had developed into a gregarious young man, was known to frequent the local pubs. As a consequence, he was eventually regarded as being a member of a group known as the "Happy Gang," made up of seminarians who were a familiar sight in the taverns of the town during their free time.

As the year unfolded, however, the young man settled down to a more sober lifestyle. He continued to apply himself to his studies throughout his second year at the seminary. Two events, occurring during the summer following his second year, also helped to moderate his exuberant behavior. The first was the sudden death on September 2nd, 1807 of his friend, Denis Duplay. The second was a serious conversation with Father Linossier, who supervised the seminary, about improving Marcellin's general conduct.

There can be little doubt that the death of his mother, Marie Thérèse, in 1810, contributed to the changes in Marcellin's behavior. She had played an important role in furthering his priestly vocation; with her death he redoubled his efforts at the minor seminary. In 1809 he had resolved, "O my Lord and my God, I promise you to no more offend you, to make acts of faith and of hope, never to return to the tavern without necessity, to avoid bad company, and to lead others to practice virtue." A year later, we find him acting on his resolve.

Early in the process of his formation as a priest, then, Marcellin became more open to the power of God's transforming grace in his life. The Lord used some very human means to focus the future saint's mind, heart, spirit, and energies on this one aim: loving Jesus and, in turn, helping others to do the same.

Marcellin's final years at Verrières

In 1810 Jean-Claude Courveille came to the seminary. This young man was to play a central role, a few years later, in the early stages of the Marist movement. Marcellin continued to struggle with self-discipline, but did not always meet with success. For example, the day after celebrating the feast of Saint Marcellin with a trip to the local tavern, he wrote, "I acknowledge, Lord, that I do not know myself yet; that I still have very great defects." Throughout his years at Verrières, however, he made confident appeals to God for help. This confidence in God was already one of the cornerstones of his spirituality.

Some time after Father Barou's arrival at the seminary as superior, Marcellin was named a monitor because of his demonstrated maturity. The task of monitor required him to watch over the dormitories and study halls. The assignment also brought with it an unexpected benefit: the young man was given the use of an alcove in the dormitory. As a consequence, he was able to study late into the night.

The year 1812-1813 was Marcellin's last at the minor seminary. Napoleon had closed many similar institutions, so student enrollment at Verrières had increased considerably. Right up until the end, Marcellin struggled with studies. His report for the last year of minor seminary confirms his lack of scholastic progress. His instructors rate his fund of knowledge as "weak." They do, however, point out that the young man had improved in a number of other areas. He is described as a "hard worker" of "good" character and as demonstrating "very good" conduct.

Marcellin passed eight difficult years at Verrières. Poorly housed and fed, he learned to endure. It was an important lesson, and one that would stand him in good stead during the years ahead. Within a few months, he would set out for the major seminary of Saint Irenaeus. To an astute observer, this much was obvious already: from an obscure corner of early nineteenth-century

France, the eventual founder of the Little Brothers of Mary was already beginning to come into his own.

St Irenaeus: the Major Seminary

Having been in existence for 150 years, the major seminary for the Lyons diocese, Saint Irenaeus, had, for most of that time, been under the direction of the Sulpician Fathers. Napoleon, however, expelled the group in 1810 because it supported the papacy. However, Sulpician influence lingered after their departure; many of the seminary professors during Marcellin's time were Sulpician-trained.

Lyons, a city located at a point where the Saône and Rhone rivers meet, is a place even to this day where devotion to Mary plays a central role in people's lives. The basilica of Our Lady of Fourvière, perched on a bluff high above the city, dominates the scene. Is it any wonder, then, that Marcellin strengthened his devotion to Mary during his years at Saint Irenaeus?

The young man spent the better part of three years at the seminary. Because of its location in Lyons, also a large and politically alert city, the students at Saint Irenaeus were interested in world events. Napoleon's harsh treatment of Pope Pius VII had shocked many of them and strengthened the pro-Pope, or Ultramontane, group within the seminary. They opposed the Gallican, or national Church, movement within French Catholicism because its adherents advocated greater freedom from Rome in spiritual affairs.

Marcellin had little interest in factionalism. He supported the primacy of the pope in spiritual affairs, but did so without resorting to extremes.

Sulpician influence

Marcellin studied theology at Saint Irenaeus, and followed a schedule largely monastic in nature. A well-ordered life was promoted, along with self-denial and conquest of the flesh.

Under the eye of the ascetic Father Gardette, the Superior, the seminarians led a life of strict regularity. Silence, recollection, prayer, self-examination, and visits to the Blessed Sacrament were emphasized. Slackness was not tolerated; the seminary rule stated clearly: "Time which is not taken up by any other exercise on the timetable is to be spent in study."

Meditation, particularly on Jesus Christ, was a central feature of the formation process. Devotion to Mary, based on the approach of the French theologians Bérulle and Olier, also occupied a place of privilege in the program. Courses dealing with dogma, scripture, liturgy, and morals took up the better part of each day.

Unfortunately, Jansenism also influenced Marcellin's study of moral theology. This heresy judged human nature to be corrupt and taught that valid forgiveness from God was hard to obtain. Jesus Christ was seen as a severe and inscrutable Redeemer. The ideas of Jansen and his followers had taken root and flourished in the Gallican Church. As a result, they influenced Marcellin's own life, though thankfully, not to a great extent.

Seminary's tranquility disturbed

Rapid political changes shook France in 1814; the ripple effects of these unfolding events found their way into the corridors of Saint Irenaeus. Napoleon abdicated on April 6th, 1814. Cardinal Fesch, his uncle, fled immediately to Italy. The Bourbons returned to the throne of France. The new King, Louis XVIII, seeking redress for the indignities that the papacy had suf-

fered at the hands of Napoleon, quickly re-consecrated the Kingdom of France to Mary, Mother of God.

The vast majority of the seminarians had positioned themselves against Napoleon. As a consequence, a great deal of political discussion occupied their time throughout 1814. One historian of the period described it as "a terrible year," one during which
seminarians spoke more of politics than theology.

Adding to the turmoil of the period was Napoleon's return
to France and to power. Cardinal Fesch, never one to miss an
opportunity that would work in his favor, seized the moment to
return to his episcopal city of Lyons, reaching it on May 26th,
1815. He stayed only three days, but was quite active during this
brief period. One day he made his way with two Vicars General
to the seminary. His mission: to check out attitudes he had heard
were prevalent there, attitudes that disturbed him.

Some of the more moderate seminarians had been writing
letters to family and friends condemning the tyrant Napoleon. The
most rabid volunteered for the "royal united troops," with head-
quarters in the nearby Forez mountains. Fesch worried that
Napoleon's police would close the seminary.

His visit was a failure. Spying his red soutane in the distance,
many seminarians disappeared, hiding in their rooms and else-
where. While the Cardinal was getting into his coach to leave,
Louis Querbes, who would later found the Clerics of Saint Viateur,
and who was known to be a "royal volunteer in a cassock," rushed
up with chalk and wrote on the side of the cardinal's carriage,
"Long live the king!"

Despite all the turmoil, political events were far from Marcellin's mind. He appeared to hold himself aloof from this type of
involvement. Why? An easy answer to this question is hard to find.
Some commentators speculate that, in light of the Revolution of
1789's impact on his family and hometown, he wanted no part of
anything resembling it. Others suggest that, for reasons of health,
he might have been living with his family in Marlhes at the time
of the unrest.

Brother Jean-Baptiste, his first biographer, disputes this last suggestion; he insists that Marcellin was in constant residence at the seminary. The young man might, however, have simply been seeking peace of mind from all the political unrest. If such was the case, he was not alone in this pursuit. Jean-Claude Colin, future founder of the Marist Fathers and a contemporary of Marcellin at Saint Irenaeus, refers to 1815 as "a wretched year."

In spite of the unrest at the seminary, Saint Irenaeus will be remembered as a remarkable place in terms of the fruit it produced. Saint Jean-Marie Vianney, the future Curé of Ars, was numbered among Marcellin's classmates.

Journey to ordination

His teachers and superiors at Saint Irenaeus held Marcellin in high regard. He had made quite a favorable impression. A brief survey of some of the young seminarian's resolutions gives an insight into his spiritual journey at this time in his life. A word, though, of warning: the spirituality of the period contributed greatly to what Marcellin wrote about himself. After all, Saint Eugène de Mazenod, a contemporary, in one self-reflection described God as "outraged by this miserable worm, this mass of rottenness!" At the outset of the nineteenth century, those later considered saints were not adverse to describing themselves as wretched people greatly in need of God's saving grace.

With that said, it is interesting to note that the practice of charity ranked high among the resolutions Marcellin made in 1815. The ever-present political disputes common at the seminary at the time no doubt played a role in the making of this resolution. We note also that the young man's preparation for priesthood led him to "deprivation of self, renunciation, a life of prayer, of rule, of study."

His resolutions for the holiday period emphasize habitual

prayer and living in God's presence. Marcellin organized his spiritual life carefully during these periods: prayer, fasting, visiting the sick, teaching young people religion. Commenting on his abilities in this last area, Julienne Epalle — mentioned earlier as a Champagnat neighbor — reported, "He taught so well that both adults and children often remained two hours without getting tired."

Marcellin judged his love of others to be an extension of his love of God. He placed great emphasis on having good family relationships, noting on at least one occasion, "I will strive to win them all to Jesus Christ by my words and example. I will not say anything that will annoy or offend them." After ordination, he would be remembered also for his fine and sensible judgment in matters of conscience. It was as a counselor, confessor, and wholehearted pastor of souls that he was so well remembered and loved by the people of La Valla, his first appointment as a priest.

It is of interest to note that Marcellin's quest for self-control does not place undue emphasis on problems with sexuality. He appears to have had a well-balanced attitude in this area. His approach stands in sharp contrast to that of many of his day. Jean-Claude Colin, for example, suffered greatly and was weighed down by excessive rigorism in the area of sexual morality. He struggled for several years before compassion for the penitent was able to overcome the harsh viewpoints instilled in him, in part, by his seminary formation.

Marist movement gets underway

The French Revolution had set off a wave of persecution against the Catholic Church. Religious orders declined rapidly in size and influence. In 1789, for example, there were approximately 2000 Benedictine monasteries in Europe; by 1815, a mere twenty were still functioning. In another example: of all the congregations of men in existence prior to the Revolution, only two — the

Jesuits and the De La Salle Brothers — ever grew again to be as large as or larger than they were prior to the Revolution.

By way of contrast, the Restoration set in motion a flood of religious activity. Many previously suppressed religious orders re-emerged; an extraordinary number of new ones sprang into existence. Father Bochard, one of the Vicars General of the Diocese of Lyons, was determined to found a new congregation. Eventually, he set up a group named the Society of the Cross of Jesus. He saw the seminary as a fertile field for gaining new recruits for his small band. In the hopes of so doing, he enlisted the unwitting aid of a seminarian, Jean-Claude Courveille.

Courveille had been born into a well-to-do family of merchants. When he came to the seminary, he brought with him a fascinating history. At age ten, for example, he had contracted a serious eye condition after a bout with smallpox. Concerned about his limited vision, his mother took her son to the shrine of Our Lady of Le Puy. There in 1809, at age twenty-two, he was allegedly cured of his blindness after oil from a sanctuary lamp had been applied to his afflicted eyes. This event led Courveille to dedicate his life to Mary. He claimed in later years to have also heard a voice on the feast of the Assumption, 1812, directing him to found the Society of Mary. The purpose of this group was quite simple: it would do for the Church of nineteenth-century France what the Jesuits had done for the Church of the sixteenth century.

Bochard was eager to speak with Courveille, especially when he learned of the young man's plan to found a religious congregation. Since, as was mentioned earlier, the former was in the process of setting up his own religious association, he thought that he could wed the two projects.

Bochard encouraged Courveille to seek members for the Marist group he had in mind. The Vicar General's motives, however, were not pure as the driven snow: he set about evaluating each of the men Courveille was considering, with an eye to their eventual membership in the Society of the Cross of Jesus.

Oblivious to the Vicar's scheme, Courveille set out on his membership drive and in a short while had fifteen recruits, among them Marcellin Champagnat. All in their twenties and thirties, they came from French peasant families. These young men spent the year 1814-1815 hammering out the fundamental principles of the new Society. It was to be made up of priests, auxiliary brothers, sisters, and lay men and women. The group of priests would form the Society's core.

Early in the discussion, Marcellin introduced the idea of establishing another branch of the Society, one made up of teaching brothers. His fellow seminarians did not express much enthusiasm for the plan. From our study of the young man's story, however, we know by now that Marcellin was a persistent soul. He kept putting forward his proposal and eventually, the others agreed: the Society of Mary would include among its number a group of teaching brothers. Responsibility for getting it started, however, was left to the young man who proposed its foundation.

How account for Marcellin's tenacity in wanting agreement that a group of teaching brothers would be part of the new Society? First and foremost, he wanted to address the widespread lack of religious education and spiritual formation found in his day. Brother Jean-Baptiste quotes him as saying, "We must have brothers to teach catechism, to help the missionaries and to conduct schools." Marcellin's dream was ambitious: to make Jesus known and loved among the young. In this undertaking, he would encourage his brothers to pay special attention to the most neglected children.

Other obvious explanations can be found in Marcellin's own personal struggles with French, his lack of academic preparation for seminary life, and the backwardness he must have felt sitting in class with younger boys, so much better prepared scholastically.

There is also a larger reality to take into account in explaining Marcellin's dream about a branch of teaching brothers. Education had collapsed in France during the Revolution. Many more schools were closed than were opened by the government. Teaching ceased to be considered an honorable profession and was left, in large measure, to those who could do little else.

In 1801, Portalis, the chief architect of Napoleon's Civic Code, made this observation, "There is no education without moral teaching and without religion." Fourteen years later, in 1815, the government finally admitted that there were too few schools in France. The Commission of Public Instruction, entrusted with the task of organizing education nationally, began to insist that every "commune take the necessary means to ensure that its local children receive primary education, and for poor children, it is free."

Some initial steps had been taken to address the country's educational crisis. Napoleon had restored the De La Salle brothers in 1803, along with orders of sisters. While Marcellin was aware of the work of the former, he knew that their efforts were concentrated on children living in urban centers. He longed to provide the same opportunities for young people in the hamlets, villages, and small towns of the hill country.

Marcellin may also have been aware of the details of the Royal Ordinance of February 29th, 1816. It provided for financial assistance to be given to those who entered the field of education. All of these elements worked together, pushing Marcellin forward. However, it would be his encounter with a young man named Jean-Baptiste Montagne that finally crystallized his dream and filled it with the urgency needed to make it a reality.

Ordination

On July 22nd, 1816, Marcellin realized his dream of many years: Bishop Dubourg of New Orleans ordained him a priest. Sharing the joy of the day and receiving the sacrament along with him were seven other members of the group now beginning to be known as the Society of Mary. The day after their ordination, the eight, accompanied by four seminarians, set off on pilgrimage to Fourvière. The basilica that fills the site today did not exist then. Instead, the group made their way to the shrine of the Black Virgin, a small chapel which the present-day basilica adjoins. Jean-Claude Courveille celebrated Mass for them. At its conclusion, all twelve renewed their pledge and dedicated their lives to Mary.

The original Marist dream called for one Society, not several. The various branches were to be subordinate to the unity of the whole. In making their pledge at Fourvière, the early Marists knew that they were committing themselves to some future action. For the present, they were subject to the authority of diocesan officials who assigned the newly ordained widely throughout the vast Diocese of Lyons. So it came to pass that Marcellin found himself on his way to the village of La Valla, located in the obscure foothills of Mount Pilat. There he took up the work of his first priestly assignment on August 13th, 1816, two days before the feast of the Assumption.

Reflection questions

Marcellin Champagnat faced many difficult challenges on his road to ordination. What similar challenges have you faced in your own life? How have they strengthened and shaped you? What means did you take to overcome them?

Looking back on this period in the life of Marcellin Champagnat, what are the qualities you most admire in the man? What about them fills you with admiration?

Chapter III

Curate and Young Founder

$\mathcal{D}$id adversity stalk Marcellin Champagnat? One must wonder. We have already seen that his road to priesthood was strewn with obstacles. In the person of Father Jean-Baptiste Rebod, pastor at his first parish in La Valla, he would encounter several others.

Rebod was an unfortunate man. Had the Church not suffered such devastation after the Revolution, he would have been counseled in the seminary to think of doing something else with his life. Instead, he was trained hurriedly, ordained, and, in 1812, appointed parish priest in La Valla.

The pastor suffered from arthritis and an unfortunate stammer, drank to excess, and did little to animate the life of the parish. When Marcellin arrived in 1816, he found both presbytery and church in disarray and neglect. When the pastor opened the door to let him in, the young curate could not help seeing a number of empty wine bottles strewn about the room. Marcellin's pastor proved to be quite a problem for his young associate.

La Valla was also not Marlhes. The terrain of the two regions differed greatly. The word La Valla, meaning valley, is actually something of a misnomer when applied to the area around Mount Pilat. Rather than being made up of stretches of good soil surrounded by hills, the locale has hardly any level ground to boast of. Ravines, rocks, precipices, and fast mountain streams, etching their way through rock and soil, are more common sights. During the young curate's time, some places were almost inaccessible for want of passable roads. Without doubt, Marcellin Champagnat faced a tough assignment in the midst of some rugged terrain.

The people of La Valla and the Revolution

The people of La Valla were lukewarm, at best, in their support for the Revolution and, hence, were not popular with the country's central government. Though the town was almost completely Catholic, during the Revolution the parish church was open only on every tenth day, and then solely to worship the Goddess of Reason, as prescribed by government decree. Parishioners did, however, gather on Sundays and feast days at the small Chapel of Our Lady of Pity, located about 500 meters from the town.

These get-togethers were interrupted suddenly on September 27th, 1793, when police arrived during the early evening as the parishioners were singing Vespers. Panic erupted when the police entered the chapel on horseback, swords drawn. A week later, two members of Saint-Chamond's Jacobin Club came to town and knocked down crosses in the local cemetery. Their actions proved to be too much for one parishioner, Jean Thibaud. He could not contain his anger and pitched very vigorously into these two scoundrels from the Club. Thibaud was arrested but subsequently released.

The then parish priest, Father Gaumond, was not so fortunate. Refusing to take the government oath required of clergy, he was hunted down, captured, and taken to Saint-Etienne. Condemned at nearby Feurs, Father Gaumond was eventually executed by guillotine.

A certain simplicity marked life in La Valla. During the summer months outdoor work occupied the entire day. Winter brought long evenings during which weaving, tool repair, and quiet moments by the fire were common pastimes. Neighbors stopped by to talk, sing or help out with chores. The family unit remained strong.

The Revolution posed a threat to this widely accepted way of living. Men were pressed to attend political meetings, spending less time at home. Some went off alone to the taverns to drink, discuss politics, read the newspapers, or listen to someone read them aloud. Cheaply printed political tracts took up the time of others. There was talk of emancipating women.

With family life breaking down, another threat to familiar and accepted ways of living appeared. Up until this time, dancing had been a favorite pastime of the mountain people. The Napoleonic armies, however, brought with them on their return from the German States, brought with them a new form of this diversion: the waltz. It quickly came under siege.

In the region's traditional dances, partners touched rarely, and then only slightly on the hand, hardly enough to stir the passions. But in the waltz, couples were required to embrace and to move together as though one.

In France the waltz was widely regarded as morally explosive. Jean-Jacques Rousseau, for example, insisted that neither his daughter nor his wife be permitted to dance it. Tellingly, the *Journal de Paris*, in its July 8th, 1807 issue, editorialized: "No dance is certainly more apt to upset women and to put fire in all their senses." At the same time, the paper is strangely silent about the waltz's effect on men!

Marcellin, in keeping with his seminary formation and the spirit of the times, probably objected strongly to this type of dancing. Brother Jean-Baptiste suggests that his opposition took the form of scheduling alternative activities to be held at the same time as those dances where the waltz was to take place.

More seriously, due to Rebod's neglect of souls, the parish community itself was in sorry shape. Greed, rivalry, and a lack of love marked social interaction. Bitter passions sowed seeds of dissension among the village inhabitants; some lost their Catholic faith. The pastor, incapable of dealing with his own personal problems, was at a loss as to what to do.

A time of Catholic revival

The abdication of Napoleon in 1814 gave rise to the restoration of the Bourbon monarchy. Under the new king, Louis XVIII, and his brother, Charles X, the Catholic Church once again received favorable treatment until 1830, when the Bourbons were forced to make a hasty retreat.

As mentioned earlier, many religious orders flourished in this more open atmosphere. New life was also breathed into parish renewal; at the church in La Valla, Marcellin took leadership in this movement.

To keep his fervor alive, the young priest set up a rigorous schedule of ascetical practices for himself. He rose at 4:00 AM and began his day with a half-hour meditation. Daily Mass was preceded by fifteen minutes of recollected prayer. Though fully engaged in parish work, Marcellin still found at least an hour each day to study theology. Fridays he fasted, and he faithfully visited the parish sick.

The practice of the presence of God was, more and more, at the heart of Marcellin's spiritual life. His path to a deeper relationship with Jesus and Mary, however, was not an easy one; the young priest encountered many rough stretches along the way.

The parish curate

Marcellin worked hard at developing an understanding heart, and with good reason. He was frequently called out to visit people at odds with one another. In these situations, his conciliatory spirit, cheerful character, and simplicity of manner worked together to foster reconciliation.

The young priest also had an uncanny knack of being able to deliver correction in a way that others found acceptable. He could admonish people without damaging their self-esteem. As a result, many came to see faults in themselves that, though previously pointed out by others, they had been unable to accept.

By necessity and temperament, Marcellin spent long hours preparing his sermons. Study, reflection, and prayer were the ingredients he put into these lessons. At first, his sermons were simple and short; the people of the parish were impressed. The young priest harmonized his instructions with the events of their everyday life. Simply put, Marcellin spoke the language of the people he was called to serve; thus, he was able to speak to their hearts.

But the new curate was at his best in the confessional. In spite of the rigorism of his seminary training, Marcellin managed to retain his compassion, good sense, and understanding of human foibles. Brother Jean-Baptiste tells us, "No words can express the kindness of heart which he showed towards his penitents. He spoke to them with tenderness and force." Marcellin had a wonderful gift for guiding souls towards God.

However, the pastor Rebod continued to be a thorn in the young priest's side. Marcellin was not merely an idle dreamer, he took action to bring his dreams to life. His initiatives, in the pastor's eyes, only upset the somnolence of parish life in La Valla. Whether threatened by Marcellin's activities, or jealous of the relationship he developed with parishioners, Rebod did not miss an opportunity to criticize his young assistant or attempt to humiliate him. Despite the pastor's antagonism, however, the curate won the hearts of those who came to pray with him or to hear him preach.

For example, one Sunday evening Marcellin was giving a short instruction at the end of Compline. The pastor suddenly appeared in the church and intoned *O crux ave*, the Latin hymn with which Compline comes to a close. The startled congregation was indignant, and so the pastor continued as a choir of one. When he had finished singing, Marcellin continued with his instruction. Later, when the young priest started his group of brothers, Rebod was one of the project's most outspoken critics. He rarely missed an opportunity to condemn it publicly or to belittle and embarrass its initiator.

Marcellin responded to Rebod with admirable self-restraint, trying by prayer and friendly advice to help the parish priest. The young curate deprived himself of wine in the hope that his example would aid the pastor. While deserving credit for helping to reduce Rebod's excessive lapses, Marcellin's interventions ultimately came to no avail. Protests against the parish priest rose steadily in frequency and volume, and continued throughout the early part of 1824. In June of that year, diocesan authorities removed Father Rebod from the parish; six months later he was dead at age forty-eight.

We must have brothers

When Marcellin arrived in La Valla two schools were operating. The Sisters of Saint Joseph had re-established their primary school for girls in 1803. The well-qualified Jean-Baptiste Galley was schoolmaster at a similar institution for boys. Unfortunately, after he married in 1818, he left for Saint-Julien-en-Jarez, and no suitable replacement was found. Jean Montmartin followed Galley as schoolmaster. At age twenty-four he was well qualified academically, holding a public teaching diploma. Unfortunately, he also drank to excess.

As was mentioned earlier, Marcellin was aware of the lack of provision for schooling in France, particularly in rural areas. A report on education in the Loire Department, where La Valla was located, had this to say about the situation, "The young are living in the most profound ignorance and are given to the most alarming dissipation."

Teachers were not held in high regard. One report described them as, "drunkards, irreligious, immoral, the dregs of the human race." Admittedly, the educational picture improved somewhat under the rule of Napoleon and more so after the accession of Louis XVIII. The Ordinance of February 1816 authorized the printing of suitable text books, the establishment of model schools, and the payment of teachers. It also gave a strong impetus to primary education: every parish was required to provide it. The children of families who could not pay were to receive free instruction. The climate was ripe for Marcellin to realize his dream.

The founder, though, was not simply concerned about providing better educational opportunities for young people. He was also preoccupied with helping to foster their religious development and experience of God's love. Marcellin was often heard to say, "I cannot see a child without wanting to let him know how much Jesus Christ loves him and how much he should, in return, love the divine Savior."

The young priest saw education as a means for integrating faith and culture. Brother Jean-Baptiste tells us, "in founding his Institute, Father Champagnat had more in mind than providing primary instruction for children, or even than teaching them the truths of religion. He said, 'We aim at something better: we want to educate the children, to instruct them in their duty, to teach them to practice it, to give them a Christian spirit and attitudes and to form them to religious habits and the virtues possessed by a good Christian and a good citizen.'"

Though two schools existed already in the parish of La Valla, the young priest did not abandon his intention of establishing a group of teaching brothers as part of the Society of Mary. He was impressed by the piety and good behavior of a twenty-two year-old parishioner named Jean-Marie Granjon, a former Grenadier in Napoleon's Imperial Guard.

On one occasion, the young man asked Marcellin to visit someone who was sick in his hamlet. The priest agreed and, as they walked together, took note of the character and disposition of the young man. So satisfied was he with Granjon's responses to his questions, that Marcellin brought the young man a copy of *The Christian's Manual* when he returned the next day to visit the sick.

Granjon refused the book initially, pointing out that he was unable to read. Marcellin was undeterred. The young curate said, "Take it just the same. You can use it in learning to read and I will give you lessons if you wish." Granjon accepted the priest's offer.

Marcellin and Jean-Baptiste Montagne

Shortly thereafter an event occurred that for Marcellin was a conclusive sign to move ahead with his dream of founding a congregation of brothers. The young priest was called to the house of a carpenter in Les Palais, a hamlet just beyond Le Bessat. A seventeen-year-old boy, Jean-Baptiste Montagne, lay dying. The lad was entirely ignorant of matters of faith. Marcellin instructed him, heard his confession, and prepared him for death. He then left to visit another sick person in the area. When he returned to the Montagne household, the young priest learned that Jean-Baptiste had died.

Marcellin's encounter with this adolescent boy transformed him. Jean-Baptiste's lack of knowledge about Jesus confirmed his belief that God was calling him to found a congregation of brothers to evangelize the young, particularly those most neglected. Walking back to the parish house in La Valla, Marcellin decided to put his plan into action: he would ask Jean-Marie Granjon to become the first member of his community of teaching brothers.

The first recruit

Jean-Marie, to be known later as Brother Jean-Marie, accepted the young priest's invitation on October 28th, 1816; he was eager to give himself to the work. Marcellin had taken the first step to found his Little Brothers of Mary. A second step followed very quickly.

A small house near the presbytery was available for purchase. Marcellin wanted to buy it, but Father Rebod, the pastor, opposed the move. However, Marcellin was able to obtain a loan for half the purchase price from Jean-Claude Courveille, now curate at nearby Rive-de-Gier, and to make up the difference from his own funds. Marcellin signed a tentative contract with Jean-Baptiste Bonner, the owner, and set to work cleaning and repairing the old building. He also built two wooden bedsteads and a small dining table. As encouraging as these developments were to Marcellin, a far more promising event came quickly: a second recruit.

The community begins to grow

Jean-Baptiste Audras, later Brother Louis, was only fourteen and a half when he asked to join the De La Salle Brothers at Saint-Chamond. Judging him to be too young, they advised him to continue discussing his vocation with his confessor. As luck would have it, that person was the young curate from La Valla. The boy told Marcellin that he had resolved to consecrate his life to God. After talking with Jean-Baptiste and his parents, and reflecting prayerfully on the situation, the priest invited young Audras to join Granjon.

Two months later the house repairs were complete. The first two recruits took up occupancy on January 2nd, 1817. Henceforth, the Bonner house would be referred to, at least in the Marist world, as the "cradle" of the Institute, and January 2nd, 1817 as the foundation date of the Little Brothers of Mary. Its members were to embrace a spirituality that included mindfulness of God's presence, confidence in Mary and her protection, and the practice of the "little" virtues of simplicity and humility.

Throughout the remaining winter months, Granjon and Audras lived together in the house. Marcellin taught his charges to read, and gave them the tools they would need to teach children. He showed them how to pray and to make nails. The latter were sold to provide an income for the community. He also quickly decided that his brothers would wear a distinctive uniform: a long black coat, black pants, a cloak, and a round brimmed hat.

Both Granjon and Audras assisted Marcellin with many of his pastoral duties. They visited and helped the aged and infirm in the hamlets, gathered wood for the needy, and brought them food regularly.

A founder educates his brothers

Marcellin engaged Claude Maisonneuve, formerly a member of the De La Salle Brothers congregation, to instruct his brothers in methods of teaching. Maisonneuve was familiar with the simultaneous method, employed in all De La Salle schools. This instructional technique, also known as the Brothers' method, had the teacher gathering together into sections students of the same level of ability. Each group was then taught successively while those in the remaining sections occupied themselves with other studies. By means of this method, classes of 50 to 70 pupils could be instructed at the same time. The young priest wanted this method of teaching to be used in schools where his brothers would teach.

Though Maisonneuve instructed Granjon and Audras in the theory and practice of teaching, Marcellin attended to their religious and intellectual formation. He was a skilled catechist and also helped them with their general education.

The young priest must have marveled at the swiftness with which the pieces needed to establish his Institute fell into place: the Montagne boy, his first two recruits, the availability of a house nearby, the proximity of qualified teachers to educate his brothers. Events did not slow down during the next several months, and, often enough, they were as unexpected in nature as the previous ones.

Jean-Claude Audras was the third recruit for the Little Brothers, his path to the Institute being an unlikely one. Charged by his parents with the task of going to La Valla to fetch home his brother Jean-Baptiste, the young man set out on his journey. However, Jean-Baptiste had no interest in returning to his family. He pleaded with Marcellin, "My brother has come to take me home, but I won't go. Will you please urge my parents to leave me alone?"

While calming the young boy, the priest also spoke with Jean-Claude, eventually convincing him that he, too, had the qualities to be a good religious. Instead of carrying out the task his parents had assigned him, Jean-Claude decided that he wanted to join his younger brother and Granjon. Apparently, his parents were agreeable because Jean-Claude became the third member of the community in December 1817. He later took the name Brother Laurent.

Over the next six months, three more recruits appeared, among them Gabriel Rivat, who would take the name Brother François and some twenty years later succeed Marcellin as Superior of the brothers. By June 1818, six young men were living in the former Bonner house in La Valla.

Gabriel Rivat merits special mention because of his prominence in the history of the Institute. Marcellin was a wonderful catechist. However, when preparing parish children for First Communion, he knew that some parents, for a number of valid reasons, did not send their youngsters to the lessons being offered. To increase attendance, he offered a reward to any pupil who brought another child to class. The children were delighted, and the plan was a great success.

One of Gabriel Rivat's older brothers brought him to catechism class. Marcellin was quickly taken with the boy's piety and intelligence; he asked his parents if Gabriel could live with the brothers so as to obtain a good education and to learn Latin. The family, being quite religious, agreed.

Though only ten when he went to live with Marcellin and his brothers, Gabriel was blessed with great intelligence and common sense. A year later, an exception having been made, he was permitted to begin his novitiate.

The ministry begins

At this time in history, schooling in France was limited generally to the winter months. Many hands were needed for work on the family farm when the weather turned fine. So it was that in May 1818, his winter assignments in the hamlets having ended, Maisonneuve was able to come to La Valla for the summer months. A school for boys and girls, not needed for farmwork, was started in the brothers' house under his direction; Marcellin's young recruits learned by observing Maisonneuve at work and by helping with the classes as they were able.

However, Maisonneuve eventually lost interest in the brothers' school in La Valla. His manner of living was also becoming a scandal to the young brothers. Marcellin told him that he must leave. Even though the position of teacher for the town school in La Valla was available, Maisonneuve lacked the necessary teaching certificate to apply. At that time in France, members of authorized religious congregations were not required to have a government diploma. As a De La Salle Brother, Maisonneuve was not in need of one. Now that he had left that congregation, he was barred from certain positions until he acquired his certificate.

With Maisonneuve's departure, Marcellin continued to operate the brothers' school, appointing Jean-Marie Granjon, the first member of the Institute, as the school's headmaster. Jean-Marie threw himself into the task with zest as he set about educating the children entrusted to him, many of whom were abandoned and orphaned. With the passage of time, the success of the brothers' efforts became obvious — too obvious for one resident of the town who did not have their best interests at heart: the parish priest, Jean-Baptiste Rebod.

Rebod tries to cause trouble

As mentioned earlier, with the departure of the highly respected Jean-Baptiste Galley, for a time headmaster of the town school for boys in La Valla, the Town Council hired Jean Montmartin, a friend of Father Rebod, to replace him. The new headmaster drank to excess; he was also a gambler. With the growing reputation of the brothers' good work at their school in La Valla, and the steadily declining regard for Montmartin's, the latter was receiving virtually no new enrollments.

Rebod was furious. He accosted Marcellin and accused him of trying to put Montmartin and his school out of business. The young priest explained that no students accepted for Montmartin's program had been allowed to transfer to the brothers' school, nor would they be without the expressed permission of Rebod. Fortunately, Montmartin decided to quit the scene at the end of the 1818-1819 academic year. The citizens of La Valla, with the exception of the Catholic pastor, breathed a collective sigh of relief.

Strictly speaking, Marcellin's first school in La Valla was illegal. Although it was set up under Maisonneuve to provide training for the young recruits of the Little Brothers, with his departure it became a rival to the existing town school administered by Montmartin.

The brothers' school in La Valla, though, was not the only one of its kind in France after the Revolution. Education was in flux; people worried about the values being taught their children. A number of towns and parishes went ahead and opened schools not in full accord with the directives coming from Paris. The young priest probably kept his school going for several reasons: to demonstrate the need for value-oriented education, the importance of a religious dimension in a school, and the necessity of having people of principle as teachers.

In any event, by the end of the winter of 1819, the brothers' school in La Valla was thriving. The brothers also continued to teach in the hamlets, and Father Allirot, who had baptized Marcellin, asked him to establish a school in Marlhes. Late in 1818, Brothers Louis and Antoine took up that challenge.

Community life begins to take shape

As the brothers' school in La Valla developed, so also did their life in community. With Marcellin's encouragement, they elected a Director, the choice falling on Jean-Marie Granjon, the oldest and first member. A daily schedule, beginning with rising at 5:00 AM followed by prayer, was agreed upon. Each brother took a turn at cooking for the group, though since the diet appears to have been limited predominantly to soup, cheese, and vegetables, culinary skills probably did not rank very high among the talents of Marcellin's young recruits.

The young priest eventually moved from the presbytery and joined his community of brothers. This change marks another decisive moment in Marcellin's spiritual journey. The eyes of faith suggest to us that, once again, the young priest unhesitatingly embraced the mission that God had in mind for him.

Though the pastor, Father Rebod, gave permission for the transfer, he warned his curate that he would soon tire of living in such poor conditions. The brothers were delighted to have Marcellin working and praying with them, eating the same food, and organizing and helping in their teacher training. Brother Jean-Baptiste points out, tellingly, that four years passed before any of Marcellin's young followers offered to tidy his room and make his bed. Whether or not the spirit of equality and fraternity had taken root in nineteenth-century France, it had begun to weave itself into the rich tapestry that would, in time, develop into the lifestyle characteristic of the Little Brothers of Mary.

A word about Father Rebod before we move on. Though he was often a cross to Marcellin, we need to adopt the curate's compassion in evaluating the man. Rebod was obviously troubled and unhappy. At the very least, he abused alcohol. In another era, assistance for these problems would have been more available to him. He might also have chosen another direction for his life. We do not know how many lives he touched in a positive way; undoubtedly, there were some. For Marcellin, though, he was often a source of tension. It is to the young priest's credit that he managed to respond to Rebod's antagonism with patience and understanding.

Money is a problem

Although Marcellin was a careful steward of funds, money was always a problem for the young community. Manual work, characteristic of the brothers, helped to cut costs. Income from the manufacture of nails, Marcellin's modest salary as curate, and the donations of a number of parishioners helped the young community keep its financial head above water.

Marcellin was also a shrewd businessman. When establishing a school outside La Valla, he insisted that it be an official school, with an agreement from the Mayor and Council. This arrangement insured a small salary of 400 francs for each brother. At the same time, the De La Salle Brothers insisted on 600 francs from the Councils of the towns in which they conducted schools. Marcellin also requested a recreation yard for the children and garden space for the brothers.

When he judged them ready, the young priest sent his followers out to the nearby hamlets, as well as to the towns of La Valla and Marlhes. They were full of fervor, fraternal affection, and apostolic zeal.

In the days ahead they would need all three. Beyond the hills surrounding La Valla, in the episcopal city of Lyons, trouble was already brewing for the young community. At the center of their difficulties would be one man, the same Vicar General who had taken such an interest in Jean-Claude Courveille's plan to establish a new religious congregation: Jean-Claude Bochard.

Reflection questions

The needs of others and their suffering often shape and transform us. How did both affect Marcellin's character, outlook on life, spirituality? How did they work together to make him the person that he became?

How have the needs and sufferings of others shaped and transformed you, made you the person you are today? How have they moved you to take action for the gospel's sake?

Chapter IV

The Institute Finds Its Footing

$\mathcal{B}$ochard was a formidable foe. Mercurial in temperament, interfering by nature, excessive in giving praise or assigning blame, he was one of three Vicars General for the Archdiocese of Lyons. Largely unpopular with the local clergy and a zealous supporter of Gallicanism, he conducted business for the absent Cardinal Fesch.

As we have seen, Bochard took an interest in Jean-Claude Courveille while the latter was a seminarian at Saint Irenaeus. He had little, if any, contact with Marcellin until he learned that the young priest had set up his society of brothers without official diocesan authorization. While this charge was true, there were also some false accusations lodged against the curate. As Vicar General in charge of all religious congregations, Bochard was determined to absorb the brothers at La Valla into his Society of the Cross of Jesus. He summoned Marcellin to the Chancery.

At first the Vicar was conciliatory, gently outlining the charges against the curate and seeking his response. Marcellin had wisely asked Brother Jean-Marie to accompany him on his visit to the Chancery. The young man's presence delivered a clear message: the brothers community had a Director, and it was not the curate from La Valla.

As the conversation proceeded, Bochard made his case for

merging Marcellin's brothers with his own Society. By the end of the meeting, the Vicar General thought he had won the day, but he was mistaken. Marcellin was more firmly convinced than ever that he was doing God's will. Not eager to respond promptly to the Vicar's offer, the curate of La Valla decided that he would, instead, follow the dictum: hasten slowly. His advisors including some highly placed archdiocesan clergy were encouraging.

Marcellin's work continued to expand: in 1822 another school opened in Saint-Sauveur, under the direction of Brother Jean-Marie. Saint-Sauveur was an important administrative center in the region, and the brothers were excited about this development. Up until this time, the brothers' schools were situated in places that were little more than villages. The addition of the school in Saint-Sauveur was yet another sign of the esteem in which the brothers and their ministry were held. But success can breed envy and opposition. This occasion proved to be no exception to that rule.

Brother Jean-Marie's difficulties

Brother Jean-Marie, Marcellin's first recruit, began to experience some personal difficulties. He had become inordinately obstinate, clinging to his own ideas about what constituted sanctity. Over time the young man developed a certain obsessiveness, resulting eventually in depression. Questions began to arise about Jean-Marie's suitability for religious life. Conditions of this nature were difficult to diagnose at the time. Jean-Marie's conduct, however, began to disturb the brothers with whom he was living. Many suggested that perhaps a fresh start in a new school would remedy his malady. Jean-Marie had, after all, been a successful headmaster in La Valla.

Difficulties also began to develop at the school in Marlhes. Father Allirot, the parish priest, wanted to exercise excessive control over the brothers assigned there; he also refused to provide them and their students with better housing. Conditions were apparently dreadful; Brother Jean-Baptiste describes the house in Marlhes as "small, damp, unhealthy." Marcellin intervened personally and demanded more suitable accommodations. Allirot would not budge. Then the young curate made a difficult decision: he withdrew his brothers from the school in his home parish. Communicating his final decision to the pastor, Marcellin wrote, "Your house is in so wretched a condition that I could not in conscience leave either the brothers or the children in it."

This incident teaches us an important lesson about Marcellin Champagnat. While a generous man, he also knew when to say, "no." Since neither he nor his brothers were overly demanding, the situation in Marlhes must have been frightful indeed. Poverty and simplicity marked the lives of his Institute's members. However, Marcellin also insisted that suitable lodging be provided for those with whose well-being he had been charged.

He realized, too, that certain elements, such as satisfactory housing, need to be in place for any educational undertaking to be effective. Marcellin was fond of saying that you could not teach children unless you loved them first. Providing adequate shelter was one way of expressing that love in action.

A vocation crisis

By February 1822 the Institute was made up of ten brothers. Their gifts varied and not all found a place in the classroom. Some possessed skills that produced needed income for the community or were more valuable for its internal management. One recruit, for example, was a skilled weaver. His trade fast replaced nail making as a means to support the brothers.

But Marcellin was worried. Vocations appeared to have dried up; he wondered if his Institute and its mission had a future. As always, he turned to Mary and made his problem hers. The young priest said, in effect: "It is your work; if you want it to flourish, you will have to provide the means for that to happen."

In March of the same year a young man sought admission to Marcellin's group. He came from a prominent family, known for it affluence and piety. The young fellow had already spent six years with the De La Salle Brothers in Saint-Chamond, but they had eventually sent him away.

After a three-day trial period, Marcellin refused to admit him to the Institute. "Will you receive me if I bring you half-a-dozen good recruits?" was the young man's response. Believing that only a miracle could bring about such a result, the priest accepted the challenge.

Two weeks later the applicant returned to La Valla with eight other young men. No doubt Marcellin was surprised. Though many in the group impressed him, he decided not to accept any of them. Why? For one reason, he knew too little about them; for another, the house lacked sufficient space to accommodate them.

The newcomers, however, equally impressed with Marcellin, pressured him to allow them to stay. The situation grows more complicated when we discover that the youths thought that they were on their way to the De La Salle novitiate when they stopped by the house in La Valla. Having been told that it was another novitiate of the same congregation, they assumed that they were being accommodated there for the evening. The group's recruiter was, indeed, a persuasive fellow.

Marcellin gathered the senior brothers of the community and sought their advice. Sensing that he believed that Providence had a hand in the group's arrival, the brothers advised admission but also recommended that the new recruits be subjected to special tests of their vocation.

Two weeks later the group's leader left; six more followed him over time. The remaining two died as Marist Brothers: Brothers Joseph Poncet and Jean-Baptiste who later became an assistant to the Superior General and Marcellin's first biographer.

The story has an additional happy ending. The eight young men had been recruited from the region of Haute-Loire, one that, to date, Marcellin had not considered for vocations. He quickly sent a recruiter to test the climate. Within six months, more than twenty applicants had come from the area. For years afterwards, Marcellin insisted that "it was Our Lady of Le Puy who sent them."

Other comings and goings

In April 1822, Inspector Guillard, from the Lyons Academy, arrived unexpectedly in La Valla. His mission? To investigate reports about the clandestine teaching of Latin. Only the Academy, a school board of sorts, could authorize such instruction; it was a privilege that that institution guarded carefully.

The inspector was disappointed to find neither students nor any evidence of the alleged Latin classes. The school year had come to a close; rumors about the Latin classes were unfounded.

Guillard, though, discovered that Marcellin had failed, to date, to seek legal authorization for the Institute he had founded five years earlier. This dereliction perplexed the inspector. When asked about it, the priest explained simply that he wanted to be sure that his Institute would survive before his seeking approbation for it. Here again we have evidence of Marcellin's realism and practicality: gaining authorization for a venture that would ultimately fail would be nothing more than an empty satisfaction.

Before leaving, the inspector made a tour of the building used by Marcellin and his brothers. He was not impressed. "We visited the home of the congregation," he reported later. "Everything there bespoke poverty, even gross untidiness." In defense of the early brothers' housekeeping skills, note that construction of a new dining room was underway, due to increased numbers, and barn alterations were in progress to provide additional dormitory space.

Have no doubt, though, Marcellin and his brothers were poor. Brother Laurent, an early and faithful disciple of the founder, described the material circumstances of that initial community this way: "We were very poor in the beginning. We had bread that was the color of the earth, but we always had what was necessary." Despite harsh conditions, the spirit of generosity and good humor that marked this first group of young recruits never failed to shine through.

Guillard was not the only visitor to judge the early brothers' situation harshly. In May 1822, ten brothers from Father Rouchon's community at Valbenoîte visited La Valla for a short stay. They had thought of joining Marcellin's Institute, but on seeing the poverty-stricken state of his brothers, they left without mentioning the purpose of their visit. In the eyes of Marcellin's recruits, their visitors were "well-instructed, rather well-dressed, had an air of refinement, and all the nuances of good society." Paradoxically, within five years Father Rouchon, now bereft of any followers, petitioned Marcellin to send some of his Little Brothers to staff the school he had set up at Valbenoîte.

Bochard again a problem

Bochard, the Vicar General, heard that eight postulants had joined Marcellin's Institute and that others were coming. The source of his information? Father Rebod, the parish priest. Fearing that, should the fledging Institute fail, he would be left with some financial responsibility for his assistant's young charges, the pastor fired off a letter to the Vicar General. Realizing that Marcellin's foundation was expanding beyond expectations, Bochard judged the time was right to make his move.

The Vicar replied to the pastor's letter. Without revealing the contents of Bochard's note, Rebod attempted to intimidate Marcellin. He suggested that non-compliance with the directives of the Vicar's letter could lead to suspension of priestly functions. When the curate finally learned the details of Bochard's message, he realized that the accusations leveled against him were false. He contacted the Vicar's office and made an appointment.

We are uncertain about the date of this second meeting between Marcellin and Bochard. In all probability it took place in November 1822. From the outset, the young priest realized that the Vicar had been kept well informed. Pointing to a map, for example, he could name the towns in which the Little Brothers were conducting schools. Bochard recommended an immediate union between Marcellin's brothers and his own Society of the Cross of Jesus, pointing out that the latter possessed legal authorization. Marcellin avoided making any commitments and took leave of the Vicar General as quickly as courtesy would allow. He knew, of course, that he had not seen the last of Bochard, nor was he finally free of his schemes.

The young priest was not completely defenseless. Bochard was but one of three Vicars, and the other two were favorably disposed toward Marcellin and his brothers. Following his second meeting with Bochard, the founder set up an appointment with Father Courbon, the Senior Vicar General.

At the outset, Marcellin spoke plainly. "You know my project," he told Courbon, " and all I have done for it. Give me your candid opinion of it. I am ready to abandon it if you wish me to do so. I desire only the will of God." The senior Vicar responded with support, saying, "I don't see why they should annoy you in this way. You are doing very useful work in training good teachers for our schools. Go on as usual; don't mind what people say."

Similar support came from Father Duplay, bursar and professor at the seminary, and from Father Gardette, its superior. The latter firmly advised the curate not to join his brothers with those of Bochard. Finally, Father Cholleton, an influential cleric who would shortly become a Vicar General, offered his support. This much was becoming clear: in future skirmishes with Bochard, Marcellin would be well-advised and well-armed. His next encounter with the Vicar General would take place about a year later. In the interim, however, another event occurred that sheds further light on the character and spirituality of the founder of the Little Brothers of Mary.

The Memorare in the Snow

In February 1823, Marcellin learned that Brother Jean-Baptiste had come down with a serious illness. Concerned about the brother's condition, the young priest, with Brother Stanislaus at his side, set out on the twenty-kilometer journey across rough countryside to visit him.

On their return trip, walking through heavily timbered territory, the two men were caught in the full fury of one of the region's snowstorms. Both were young and energetic, but hours of wandering lost on the slopes of Mount Pilat led eventually to exhaustion. Stanislaus reached the limits of his stamina. Night set in; the possibility of death in the snow increased with each passing hour. Both men turned to Mary for help and prayed the Memorare.

Within a short while, they spied a lighted lamp, not too far in the distance. A local farmer, Mr. Donnet, had left his house to enter a nearby stable. This particular evening, though, he took an unusual route, especially with the storm underway. Usually, he entered the stable through a convenient door in the wall of his house. For reasons that can be explained only by faith, this particular night he chose a route that took him outdoors with his lantern to brave the wind and snow. For the rest of his days, Marcellin saw his deliverance and that of Brother Stanislaus as an act of Providence, henceforth referred to as the Memorare in the Snow.

Marcellin's spirituality

For some time now, we have been following unfolding events in the life of Marcellin Champagnat. What insights do they offer us into the man and his spirituality? Without hesitation, we can conclude that he faced some formidable challenges along the way: lack of adequate preparation for seminary studies, academic difficulties, a troubled and troubling pastor, an ambitious Vicar General. Each predicament shaped him, fine tuning in him the virtues of charity, optimism, resourcefulness, and political acumen.

The episode that came to be known as the Memorare in the Snow opens another window on the man and his spirituality. What caused Marcellin to set out on his journey in the first place? Concern for a sick brother. The founder's great love for the early brothers was one of his most memorable qualities. Marcellin's world might have been small when compared to that of many people today. There was nothing small, however, about his heart. He lived a practical Christianity; love always translated itself into concrete action. A brother was sick; the founder set out to visit him.

With that said, though, we might wonder what possessed the young priest to begin his return journey in the face of a threatening snowstorm? Did he have pressing business at home, or was his knowledge of the area's terrain such that it filled him with a sense of false confidence? Some would, after all, judge the founder's return journey from Bourg-Argental to be an act of imprudence. While we would not characterize him as rash, we know by now that Marcellin took calculated risks.

Whatever other reasons motivated the timing of his return journey, we can speculate that his confidence in God's presence and reliance on Mary's protection caused him to undertake the trip where others might hesitate. His recourse to the Memorare in the face of danger was not the final effort of a dying man. Marcellin was aware of God's continual and powerful presence; Mary had also come through for him often enough that he counted on her protection without question. The Memorare in the Snow was simply an external manifestation of the much deeper spiritual reality of the man.

A knock-out blow for Bochard

Bochard decided to increase the pressure on Marcellin. At the close of the priests' retreat in August 1823, the Vicar General threatened to close the brothers' house and place ecclesiastical sanctions on the young priest, including his removal from the parish of La Valla, unless he agreed to unite his Institute with Bochard's group. The curate moved into action, relying on his friends in high places. They encouraged him to stand firm.

The Vicar employed drastic methods to break Marcellin's resistance. Father Dervieux, parish priest in the nearby town of Saint-Chamond, prompted by Bochard, attacked Marcellin, pointing out that his young recruits would be left without support should their house be closed.

Father Rebod also rose to the occasion, and attempted publicly to humiliate his curate once again. He offered to hire the brothers himself, or to arrange for their admission to other congregations, if they would renounce the founder. However, the defection of Jean-Louis Duplay, a local priest who, up until this time, served as Marcellin's confessor and spiritual advisor, proved to be the greatest blow the young priest suffered. Influenced by biased reports about Marcellin, Duplay refused to continue to advise him.

What was Marcellin's response to these developments? Initially he had some doubts and thought of setting out for the missions in America. He reasoned that he could bring the brothers with him on his journey across the Atlantic. Marcellin asked them what they thought. Their response? They were with him regardless of the decision he made.

The young priest's strategy began with a nine-day period of fasting and prayer. He also made another pilgrimage to La Louvesc and the tomb of his favorite saint, John Francis Regis.

Next, he continued to open schools. In 1823, no fewer than three were established. Marcellin consoled himself with the knowledge that he had the solid support of some diocesan authorities and a number of his fellow priests. Within a short period of time, however, the winds would shift decisively in his favor because of a most unexpected development.

A new archbishop for Lyons

In 1823 Leo XII was elected pope, following the death of Pius VII. On December 23rd, 1823, he appointed Archbishop Gaston de Pins as apostolic administrator of the archdiocese of Lyons. The days of absentee governance at the hands of Cardinal Fesch's assistant, Vicar General Bochard, had come to an end.

Bochard opposed the Pope's appointment of Archbishop de Pins, protesting it vehemently during a plenary session of the archdiocese's clergy. Refusing to have anything to do with the new administration, he set about destroying church records, including the financial statements of the archdiocese and those of the minor seminaries at Alix, L'Argentière, and Verrières.

Bochard eventually transferred from Lyons to the diocese of Belley. His departure lifted a great weight from the shoulders of Marcellin and his brothers. Though the now former Vicar General continued to question the legality of de Pins' appointment, his move to another diocese rendered him harmless when it came to the affairs of the Archdiocese of Lyons. Bochard died in 1834 at the age of seventy-five. He left behind a society of priests, sisters, and brothers. With the passage of time, these groups either faded from the scene or were absorbed into other congregations.

Is our picture of Vicar General Bochard too one-sided? Perhaps. He was, after all, a man of great energy and zeal. He was also called to serve as a leader during a complicated period of history marked by great civil and religious unrest. In his own way he thought he was furthering the Kingdom of God. However, we need to be grateful that the Vicar General lacked the power to order Marcellin to abandon his efforts. Bochard could threaten, but fortunately for the curate from La Valla and us all, he could not force compliance.

In late March 1824 Marcellin traveled to Lyons to meet with the new Archbishop. There, in the presence of several clerical friends and supporters, de Pins gave the young priest the archdiocese's blessing, a word of encouragement, and some financial aid to further his work. An historian of the period tells us that, following his meeting with the Archbishop, Marcellin went to Notre Dame de Fourvière (that small chapel where the first Marists had pledged their lives to Mary) and spent a long time at Mary's altar — utterly overcome.

Building Notre Dame de l'Hermitage

By 1824, Marcellin's Institute had grown to such an extent that he needed the assistance of another priest. The Archiepiscopal Council voted on May 12th to send Father Courveille to help out.

The priest's arrival gave Marcellin time for a project that had long been close to his heart: the construction of a building spacious enough to house the ever-increasing number of brothers. He purchased a piece of property, five acres in size, in a sheltered section of the valley of the Gier River. Bounded on east and west by steep mountain slopes, it contained a grove of oak trees and was well irrigated by water from the river. Late in May, Vicar General Cholleton blessed the cornerstone; construction was soon underway.

Marcellin and his young brothers worked steadily throughout the six months of summer and early autumn in 1824. They quarried and carried the stones for the building, dug sand, made mortar, and assisted the professional tradesmen, who had been hired for the skilled work. Lodged in an old rented house on the opposite bank of the Gier, the group came together for morning Mass in a small shed in an oak grove. This spot came to be known as the Chapel in the Woods. A chest of drawers served as the altar; a bell, suspended from a tree branch, called the community to prayer. What heady days for all involved! The young men found support in one another; they were also proud of their achievement.

Throughout construction of the five-story building, the founder set an example for his brothers. He was the first to start work each day and the last to put it aside at night. While the brothers appreciated Marcellin's efforts, some of his fellow clergy were less enthusiastic. They did not take kindly to the sight of a priest wearing dusty clothing, whose hands were rough from manual labor.

Some were quite vocal in their criticism. "Has this fool Champagnat lost his reason?" they questioned. Marcellin's parishioners, though, stood by him. They loved him as a pastor of souls, and, being working people themselves, they admired him as a laborer and builder.

The new building was ready for occupancy by the end of winter 1825. In May of that year, the brothers from La Valla took up residence at Notre Dame de l'Hermitage. Marcellin now had a Mother House for his Institute.

Throughout the period of construction the founder did not neglect the formation of his brothers. Until October 1824, he also continued to fulfill his duties as parish curate. Despite his fatigue after a day of construction work, Marcellin continued the brothers' religious and professional education. He spent his evenings instructing them about religious life and advancing their formation as teachers.

Several new foundations were established during 1824. After a wait of two years Father Gauché, parish priest of Chavanay, finally welcomed two brothers. The school they established received the wholehearted support of the parishioners; they insured that all their school-aged children would pass through its doors.

At the same time, Father Courveille intervened to help set up the brothers' school in Charlieu. The three brothers sent there found the children in a deplorable state of ignorance. However, in time, this school became one of the most flourishing early foundations of the Institute.

In addition to building the Hermitage, Marcellin was eager to gain authorization for his Institute. He pursued this goal relentlessly, but without success, for the rest of his days. In January 1825, he drew up Statutes and submitted them to the appropriate archdiocesan authorities, who then set about negotiating with the government of the new King, Charles X. Unfortunately, the King's Council of State had become more and more reluctant to authorize religious educators, especially those from congregations of men.

The Council sent Marcellin's Statutes back, demanding that several be amended. The founder's provision that his brothers take vows following their novitiate, for example, was a stumbling block. Marcellin was unwilling to accept the recommended changes. He paid a high price for his refusal to acquiesce. The founder's ongoing struggle for authorization sorely tried his patience and sapped his strength.

Courveille a problem

Because Courveille fancied himself to be the Superior of the Marists, he began to intrude into the brothers' affairs. His first concern was their style of dress. Earlier, Marcellin had established a specific attire for his community members. Courveille altered those directives; he prescribed a coat of sky blue color, covered by a blue cape. This innovation led local people to call Marcellin's recruits the "Blue Brothers." To this day, the description is used, from time to time, around Saint-Chamond. At a later date, the founder did away with both the sky blue coat and blue cape.

Marcellin was busy at this time, so he tolerated Courveille's interference. The latter developed a first Prospectus for the brothers and submitted it to Vicar General Cholleton for approval. That endorsement was granted in July 1824. The final copy of the Prospectus narrowed down the range of apostolic endeavors that Marcellin had proposed in an earlier draft. Fortunately, it also omitted most of Courveille's harangues against secular teachers, and his declarations of loyalty to the Bourbon monarchy. Of note is the fact that the Prospectus contains the first official reference to the Little Brothers of Mary.

While charismatic, Courveille was high-handed and often lacked judgment. His dealings with the town authorities in Charlieu demonstrate both facts admirably. Permitted by Marcellin to help establish a school there, Courveille was quick to request of the town government that a center for missionary priests also be established. In addition, he asked that a brothers' novitiate be built. At the same time the founder was toiling to build such a structure at the Hermitage!

As difficult as Courveille's behavior proved to be, the situation paled in comparison to what Marcellin would have to face when they all moved to the Hermitage.

Reflection questions:

Marcellin was aware of God's presence and relied completely on Mary. After reading about his life thus far, are there other aspects of his spirituality that are apparent to you? If so, what are they and how did they develop in the man?

Does your personal spirituality resemble Marcellin's in any way? If so, just how?

Chapter V

Continuing Adversity

$\mathcal{I}$n May of 1825, Marcellin, along with Courveille, twenty brothers, and ten postulants moved to the Hermitage. A monastic flavor permeated the place, aiding the brothers' spirit of recollection. In August of the same year, Father Dervieux, parish priest of Saint-Chamond, presided at the official dedication of the chapel, assisted by several other members of the local clergy.

Later in the month, the Archdiocesan Council asked Father Terraillon, another of the aspiring Marists of the Fourvière pledge, to help with the religious instruction of the brothers. Terraillon accepted the post reluctantly. Writing to his friend Jean-Claude Colin at Belley, he confessed, "If it were within my power, you would see me arriving as soon as possible in your little valley." Marcellin, in the eyes of others, now had two priests assisting him, Terraillon and Courveille. Distant rumblings, however, were already sounding in this seemingly tranquil landscape.

Jean-Claude Courveille was an unpredictable man. He had, by this time, assumed the title "Superior of the Marists." He had also managed to alienate himself from the Archdiocesan Council. They judged as excessive his work directing some of the Sisters of Mary and his efforts to found a Marist Third Order. He was told to cease and desist in these endeavors, and to confine himself to his work with the brothers. In truth, Courveille's arrogance was probably the factor that estranged many Council members from him.

Feeling reined in, the priest decided to assert himself as the Superior of the brothers. Summer had arrived; they had all assembled at the Hermitage. Courveille gathered the brothers together and delivered a lengthy address, concluding with these words: "It is necessary that you choose one of the Fathers here to direct you [that is, Terraillon, Courveille, or Champagnat]. I am ready to sacrifice myself for you."

The brothers wanted no part of his offer. Asked to write on a piece of paper their choice for Superior, they selected Marcellin. Fearing that his brothers had given insufficient reflection to the matter, or perhaps because he regarded Courveille as the Superior of the group of Marist congregations, the founder asked them to vote a second time. The outcome of the balloting? Marcellin once again.

Courveille, though, was not put off so easily. In November 1825, when the founder was visiting the brothers' schools, he assumed the role of Superior while Marcellin was away. Seconded by Terraillon, he also criticized those at the Hermitage who spoke of the absent Father Champagnat as Superior.

To emphasize his position as Superior, Courveille composed a set of rules and insisted that they be read in each community. He also took to wearing a long ornate blue cloak, fancying himself an abbot. Viewing these developments, the more caustic brothers were unsparing in their criticism.

Marcellin falls seriously ill

The day after Christmas 1825, Marcellin fell ill. Within the week death appeared imminent. Despite two months of unusually severe weather, the young priest had continued to push himself, visiting the ten scattered communities of brothers. Several other concerns weighed heavily upon the man: Courveille's increasing unacceptability to the brothers, financial difficulties, and the opening of a new school at Ampuis.

Courveille quickly sent a letter to all the brothers' communities asking for prayers for the founder. Even here, though, he managed to alienate himself further from the group, signing himself Priest, Founder, and Marist Superior General.

Some of Marcellin's creditors, alarmed by news of his illness, demanded immediate payment. The founder, preparing for the worst, made his will on January 6th, 1826. Unfortunately, the only inheritance he could pass on was debts. Not many were lining up to be heirs to such a legacy. Marcellin and his brothers suffered greatly during this period; Courveille and Terraillon were of little help. In 1833, in a letter to Vicar General Cholleton, the founder wrote this moving description of the situation: "During a long and serious illness, when heavy debts hung over my head, I wished to make Father Terraillon my sole heir. He refused my inheritance, saying that I had nothing. With Father Courveille, he did not cease to say to the brothers, 'The creditors will come very soon to drive you out of here. We will move off to a parish and leave you to yourselves.'"

Brother Stanislaus decided to contact both archdiocesan authorities and the creditors. As a result, Father Dervieux, parish priest in Saint-Chamond, assumed the founder's debts. Father Verrier, a friend since the seminary, also stepped in to help.

A will was written, containing the following provisions: should Marcellin die, the archdiocese would pay what was owed to Fathers Courveille and Verrier. It would also take possession of all real estate and other assets held in the Institute's name. The archbishop, by this time, was a patron of the brothers; undoubtedly he already thought of the Institute as an archdiocesan organization.

Marcellin recovers

The founder recovered from his illness, though it permanently weakened his constitution. By February 1826 he was back conducting business. With Courveille, he purchased a half-acre block of land, thus consolidating the Hermitage property. On March 15th, he petitioned the archdiocese for permission to establish a silk mill; its output would be another source of income for the community. Marcellin's business sense, optimism, way with people, and confidence in God's presence and providence all worked together to inspire others to give or lend him money for the works he undertook. While he was conscientious about paying his debts, he never appeared unduly concerned about money.

But the founder's sickness had taught him an important lesson. "At last," he wrote, "God, in his mercy, alas, perhaps in his justice, restored my health. I saw that in this occurrence neither the one nor the other [that is, Courveille and Terraillon] had for my young people the sentiments of a father."

Courveille, as mentioned above, had taken charge during the founder's sickness; by this time, his behavior was driving the brothers mad. He expected the novices to follow all his orders without question. They were so numerous and restrictive that they squelched any of the natural liveliness of youth. Courveille also refused to hear complaints, seemingly indifferent to the fact that young brothers were abandoning their vocation. Marcellin, still confined to bed, pleaded with Courveille to be indulgent and paternal in directing the brothers. He was wasting his breath; the request fell on deaf ears.

Fueled by ambition and jealous of the brothers' love for Marcellin, Courveille set about to discredit him with archdiocesan authorities. He presented to the archbishop a list of complaints about the founder. Father Cattet, a Vicar General, was sent to the Hermitage to investigate.

Cattet was not pleased with what he found. Marcellin was,

by this time, no longer confined to bed but convalescing at Father Dervieux's rectory in Saint-Chamond. The Vicar ordered the priest to give more time to instructing the brothers, forbade him to undertake any further building projects, and insisted that he devote himself less to material things. On returning to Lyons, Cattet also drew up a plan to merge Marcellin's brothers with the recently founded Brothers of the Sacred Heart of Father Coindre. The latter was not pleased with the idea. The archbishop, though still concerned about the Institute's precarious financial situation, did not support Cattet's plan either. When Coindre died suddenly, the Vicar General resurrected his scheme. On August 8th, 1826, however, the archbishop's Council decided to oppose any union.

Courveille s attempt to discredit Marcellin placed further strain on their relationship and damaged even more the one he had with the brothers. Shortly thereafter, an incident occurred that marked the end of Jean-Claude Courveille's association with the Little Brothers of Mary.

Courveille falls from grace

We have seen that Jean-Claude Courveille was the source of considerable difficulty for Marcellin and his young community. He was also a more troubled man than was first apparent, with significant psychological and moral limitations. Shortly after Cattet's apostolic visitation, Courveille sexually abused one of the postulants at the Hermitage. Father Terraillon, on learning of the situation, reported it immediately to Father Barou, a Vicar General. Necessary action had to be taken: Courveille was to leave the Hermitage immediately. He went to the Cistercian Abbey at Aiguebelle, 120 kilometers to the south.

While Terraillon reported the incident of abuse to Father Barou, he did not discuss it with Marcellin. Consequently, when Courveille wrote the latter in June 1826 pleading to return to the

Hermitage, the founder gave consideration to the request. He consulted with Terraillon, who was adamant: Courveille was not to return.

Who was Jean-Claude Courveille? We have seen that since ordination he had been active in encouraging groups of religious to establish themselves. He also attempted to set up a house for priests at Charlieu. He clearly considered himself to be Superior General of the Marists.

Despite his efforts and eminence, however, Courveille did not have the backing of some prominent Marists. Sometime between 1822 and 1824, Jean-Claude Colin, for example, came to the conclusion that Courveille was not the man to lead the Society. He dropped the latter's name from all correspondence he had with Church authorities.

Marist Father Stanley Hosie, a biographer of Father Colin, painted this rather unflattering portrait of Courveille, "Gifted with unusual charm and honeyed tongued, Courveille could have been almost anything he wanted to be if he had been persistent. He was not. Having begun the Society of Mary, he was content to leave the spadework to the Champagnats and the Colins. Courveille called them his 'agents.' He saw nothing incongruous in having agents who did the menial, everyday tasks for the 'Superior General,' and he played the role magnificently in his Marist religious habit: a top hat, a sweeping sky-blue coat, and a swaggering cane."

Courveille eventually found some peace at the Benedictine Abbey of Solesmes. Accepted there in 1836, he led an exemplary life for thirty years and died as a monk. However, he never forgot the Society of Mary; to the end he claimed to be its founder.

More upheavals

With Courveille's departure, did life settle down at the Hermitage? Unfortunately not. Financial problems persisted, though others appeared to worry about them more than Marcellin. The founder's optimism about money, however, was not enough to stop departures from the Institute. Courveille had convinced a few brothers that, with mounting debt, Marcellin's project was doomed to fail. He lured two or three others away to join him in still another religious foundation he set up in the diocese of Grenoble.

Brother Jean-François, one of Marcellin's early followers and a brother dear to his heart, left the Institute at this time, as did Jean-Marie Granjon, his first recruit. The latter had tried his hand at monastic life, spending a brief period at La Trappe in 1822. On his return, Marcellin appointed him headmaster at Saint-Symphorien-sur-Coise. A year later he returned to La Valla and then to the Hermitage. At the end of the brothers' retreat in 1826, the founder offered Jean-Marie a choice of two possible assignments, but he refused both, protesting that he did not want any position of responsibility. He was restless and unable to settle down.

By this point, Jean-Marie's concept of holiness had also led to some unhealthy practices. He wore hairshirts, scourged himself, and prayed for hours in cold, wintry conditions with his arms outstretched. Many brothers feared that he had become mentally unbalanced. Reason failed to make any headway. By the end of October 1826, Jean-Marie was gone.

Father Terraillon departed in the same year. He had been unhappy for a long time, and took the occasion of an invitation to preach a series of Jubilee sermons to make his escape. Marcellin was saddened by his leaving, the brothers less so. Many had had their difficulties with him. Terraillon was later a member of the first group of Marist Fathers to pronounce vows in 1836; he also became an Assistant General to Father Colin.

If 1826 was a low point for Marcellin, it did little to dampen his zeal or shake his faith and confidence in God. He opened no fewer than three new schools. Those already operating were enjoying unprecedented success. The Prefect of the Loire also visited the Hermitage. Subsequently, he gave permission to establish a cemetery on the property and made a financial grant available. A letter from Jean-Claude Colin, founder of the Marist Fathers, was another source of consolation. Dated December 5th, 1826, it read, in part: "I cannot adequately admire the blessings which God has given to this most interesting and necessary work of forming young people."

Marcellin worked to help the brothers maintain their fervor and their sense of poverty. If 1826 had been a difficult year for him, it was no less so for them. The founder was more than anxious to have another priest for the Hermitage. At the urging of Father Barou, Vicar General, Archbishop de Pins asked the newly ordained Father Séon to help out. He was more than eager to do so.

A community of Marist Fathers for Lyons

The Hermitage was now a community made up of forty-two brothers, ten novices, and two priests. Séon quickly set about his work and was a great help to Marcellin, who, until this time, had been superior, teacher, confessor, guide, and bursar for the group. The young priest also confided in the founder his hopes that the Society of Marist priests would soon be established and that he could become a member. Marcellin counseled patience; experience caused him to doubt that such a Society would emerge at any time soon.

The idea of delay upset Séon, and he thought of leaving the Hermitage to join Father Colin and the group he had gathered in Belley. But Séon quickly found that a move from one diocese to another was a difficult matter to arrange. The young priest remained at the Hermitage and helped Marcellin recruit two other priests, Jean Bourdin and Jean-Baptiste Pompallier; both had some interest in the Marist cause.

Growth continues

In 1827, ten new postulants were received and two new schools opened, at Valbenoîte and Saint-Symporien-d'Ozon. With the Institute's continued growth, and with some government support money for the brothers' schools forthcoming, Marcellin's mind turned once more toward gaining official authorization for his Institute. In this endeavor he was again disappointed. Even though Archbishop de Pins traveled to Paris, where he attempted to gain the King's approval for the Marist Brothers, powerful forces in the government, opposed to religious schools, blocked the authorization.

Marcellin's Statutes were, once again, judged unsatisfactory. Religious vows were the source of difficulty. The opponents of religion regarded vows as contrary to the Revolution's spirit of liberty. They were determined not to take any action that might encourage them. Despite this setback, the Institute continued to grow.

More trouble in the ranks

After the difficulties of 1826, Marcellin must have breathed a sigh of relief that 1827 was shaping up to be an exceptionally quiet year. His tranquility was soon shattered over, of all things, clothing!

With Courveille's departure, Marcellin changed the blue outfit that the former had prescribed for the brothers. They were now to wear a black cassock and cloak, a black woolen cord, and a white rabat. A three-cornered hat completed the outfit. A crucifix was also worn by those with perpetual profession. During the annual retreat of 1828, Marcellin introduced further changes, the first being the substitution, on the upper part of the cassock, of hooks and eyes for buttons. The lower part of the cassock would be sewn together. Most welcomed this modification.

A second change in dress introduced by the founder met with an entirely different response. Until this time, the brothers had worn wool or cotton socks. They were both comfortable and dressy. Later some brothers took to wearing silk socks, dressier still. For a number of reasons, the founder wanted to introduce socks made of serge material. Objections arose immediately: serge was too hot, hurt the feet, did not fit well. A few brothers became quite agitated; they decided to contact two Vicars General from the diocese, scheduled to visit the Hermitage the next day. Their plan was thwarted, however, when the two Vicars were recalled suddenly to Lyons. A few senior brothers, fearing that matters were now getting out of hand, sought the founder and brought him up to date.

Marcellin faced a dilemma. Being a person of prayer, he asked for God's guidance in the matter. He next set about to dissuade the dissenters. All but the hard-core were won over. The issue, though, was no longer socks; it had become obedience and morale. The founder decided to test the loyalty of those who continued to object.

All but two brothers eventually came into line. These two were men of great teaching ability and influence, but had grown slack as religious. At the previous retreat, for example, Marcellin had taken both to task for their numerous unnecessary absences from community and other unauthorized comings and goings. The founder used the present opportunity to warn both of them again about their obligations. His efforts were of little use; by October of the following year, both had left the Institute.

What can we make of this seeming tempest in a teapot over socks! Marcellin was a son of the Revolution. He opposed elegance in dress, and with good reason. After all, at the time of the Revolution many clergy were suspect because of their intimate relationship with the aristocracy.

From a religious point of view, Marcellin also wanted to reinforce a spirit of poverty. The early brothers did not have an easy life materially. The deprivation they suffered, however, bound them one to another and caused them to share what little they had. It also kept them mindful of their need to live close to the circumstances of those whom they were called to serve.

The founder might also have been trying to reinforce the lines of authority within the Institute. He was not an autocratic man, often consulting widely before taking a decision. He knew, too, that change is difficult for just about everyone: new ways are suspect; many people accept innovation only with reluctance. But Marcellin also realized that excessive individualism destroys the spirit of sacrifice and cooperation within any group. He wanted to ensure that it would not find too comfortable a home among the Little Brothers of Mary.

The end of a decade

The Institute continued to flourish. Schools opened at Feurs and Millery in 1829. During the same year, the brothers adopted a new method for the teaching of reading. Esteem for their work grew.

As the decade came to a close, the founder must have looked back with satisfaction on much that had transpired. He had recently purchased additional land in the vicinity of the Hermitage; archdiocesan officials had given approval for the profession and renewal of vows within the community; his Institute had gained the esteem and support of local authorities; and rumor had it that the archbishop was interested in helping to establish the Marist Fathers. In the midst of all this good news, and with a new decade about to unfold, Marcellin may have thought that most of his difficulties were behind him. But the soon-to-start French Revolution of 1830 would cause him, sadly, to revise that assessment.

Reflection questions

Marcellin faced disappointments, near fatal sickness, the manipulations of Vicar General Bochard, a troubled and difficult pastor, the departure of early recruits. He must have had enormous inner resources to come through these trials. From what you know about Marcellin thus far, what might those inner resources be? How did they sustain him?

What inner resources do you draw on to face challenges in your own life? What can you do practically to deepen those resources?

Le Rosey: The birthplace of Marcellin Champagnat. Photo by Nito Moraldo.

La Valla: The "Brotherhood Table" made by Marcellin for the first brothers.
Photo by Nito Moraldo.

The Hermitage. Photo by Nito Moraldo.

The urn containing the remains of St. Marcellin Champagnat
at the Hermitage.

Marcellin prayed often before this statue of Mary who "had done everything among us."

Marie a tout fait chez nous

La Valla: The brothers' school is just beyond the church and above it in this photo.

Le Rosey: Marcellin's home parish.

Marlhes. Founded in 1789.

A view of the Hermitage from above.

Lyons: The Basilica of Fourvière.

Rome: A detail of the mural by Goya depicting the Marist Family
and the spirituality of St. Marcellin Champagnat.

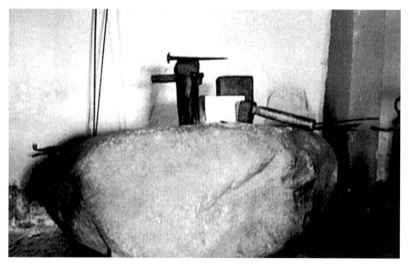

La Valla: The workshop where the brothers fabricated nails to support themselves.

"We believe that… a preferential option for the poor is a Gospel imperative" (Solidarity, 9). Photo by Henri Vignau.

The Hermitage: A stained glass window depicting the "Memorare" in the snow.

The Hermitage: A stained glass window showing Marcellin as
catechist in Le Rosey.

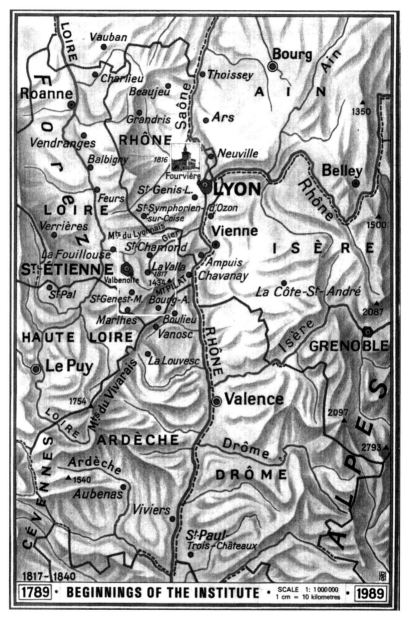

Map showing the area in which the brothers of the Society of Mary
had their origin.

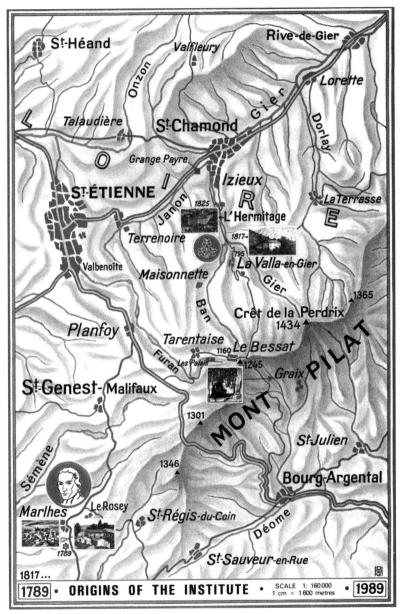

A detail of the map on page 10 indicating the relative location of
the first foundations.

"Living stones of the Father's tenderness." Photo by Henri Vignau.

"We help young people to become responsible for their own formation" (C. 88). Barcelona, Spain. Photo by Luís Serra.

"With your help, this refoundation will succeed." Photo by Henri Vignau.

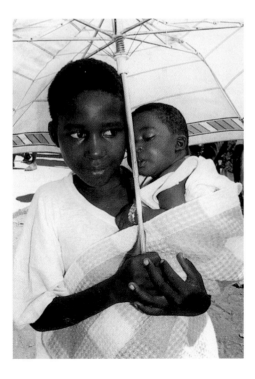

"Behind their suffering, faces hide the face of Jesus" (Message, 6). Photo by Marcel Popalier.

"We feel ourselves called... to rediscover the Montagne experience by fidelity to Christ and to the Founder (Solidarity, 10). Almofala, Brazil. Photo by Ivo de Souza.

Les Avellanes, Spain: Statue of St. Marcellin Champagnat and children.

Rome: Visit of Pope John Paul II to the College of San Leone Magno.

Chapter VI

Growth Continues

*H*istory can be whimsical. Just look at France at the outset of the nineteenth century. Napoleon fell from power in 1814, and was exiled to the island of Elba. The European powers that defeated him held the Congress of Vienna, a peace meeting at war's end, and quickly restored the Bourbon monarchy. However, they made some concessions to principles of democracy: the monarch, no longer an absolute ruler, had to contend with a Parliament. Unfortunately for history, that first one was elected on the basis of a limited franchise that favored the influential. With the Revolution of 1830, this arrangement came to a fast and final end.

By that year, the number of opposition Deputies in the Parliament about equaled those of the royalist group. A strong spirit of anti-clericalism existed among the former. Why? Because many clergy were rabidly royalist; they wanted to return to the days before 1789.

The field of education was a common and constant battleground for these two groups. Marcellin's petition for authorization of his Institute was caught in the crossfire. In early June 1830, both Archbishop de Pins and the founder had high hopes that they would gain the long sought-after legal recognition for the Little Brothers of Mary. Those hopes were dashed when parliamentary elections, held in the same month and fueled by anti-clericalism, resulted in a landslide victory for the king's opponents. A series of events followed that led to the expulsion from France of the Bourbon King Charles X.

Despite the election's results, the Great Powers of Europe would not allow a republic to be established. Instead, they set up a conservative government under a new king from the Orleans branch of the royal family. Though more indifferent than antagonistic to religion, the government followed a policy of anti-clericalism. Many Catholics in prominent government positions resigned. Marcellin's request for legal recognition for his Institute fell victim to these developments.

The revolution of 1830 fueled tensions between Church and State. Frightened members of the clergy stopped wearing their religious garb, trying to be as inconspicuous as possible. Marcellin counseled the brothers to stay above the fray, put their faith in God, and redouble their zeal for the education of young people and for their Christian instruction.

The founder appeared unshaken by all the upheaval. In August 1830 he welcomed postulants into the Institute and clothed them with the religious habit. Asking Mary's special protection during a difficult time of political and social unrest, he introduced the Salve Regina as the first community prayer of the brothers' day, a custom that continues to the present.

Difficult days

With the passage of time anti-clericalism grew. The seminaries at Metz, Lille, and Nîmes were sacked. Despite these developments, the brothers continued to wear their cassocks in public. This fact, coupled with knowledge that Archbishop de Pins, a royalist, was well disposed to Marcellin, gave rise to rumors about the founder. Reports circulated that the Hermitage was filled with arms, and that the brothers took part in daily military drills and were harboring a counter-revolutionary leader. On July 31st, 1831, the Crown Prosecutor and a company of troops appeared at the door of the Hermitage to investigate.

Pushing their way into the house, they met a hastily summoned Marcellin. He greeted the Crown Prosecutor with these words: "A great honor for us, I assure you. I see you are not alone. I know what you want. Make a thorough search, so that you will find out for sure whether we have any nobles or other suspected persons hidden here, or any weapons." Then, starting with the cellars, he took the Prosecutor and troops through the entire building.

The visitors ardor soon cooled, and they suggested cutting short the search. Marcellin would not hear of it. He insisted on a thorough inspection. With that completed, however, he invited the Prosecutor and those with him to have something to eat and drink. All accepted this offer of hospitality. As the Crown Prosecutor left, he turned to the priest and said, "I promise you this visit will be for your good."

True to his word, the Prosecutor's report refuted the rumors that had circulated about the Hermitage. He also praised Marcellin and the work of his brothers.

Though the danger of violence and vandalism subsided a few months after the outbreak of the Revolution of July 1830, the founder advised the brothers to make their annual retreat locally in their own houses. He wanted to minimize the possibility of property damage in the brothers' absence; he was also prepared to challenge any replacement of brothers with lay teachers while the brothers were away from their schools. Remember: the Institute still did not have approval, and the new government was hardly well disposed. Marcellin Champagnat was a very practical and politically astute man.

Additional developments

The prominence of the Society of Mary grew in the Archdiocese of Lyons. The Archbishop's Council named Marcellin superior for the group there, and assigned Father Jacques Fontbonne to the Hermitage as an additional chaplain. About the same time, the priests in the Lyons and Belley dioceses who were associated with the Marist movement elected Jean-Claude Colin as overall superior for the Marist Fathers.

Marcellin had been developing a Rule for his brothers since 1817. Early copies were handwritten and the text revised with the opening of each new foundation. When writing the Rule, the founder used a method of broad consultations: the most experienced among the senior brothers were invited to reflect upon, discuss, and give feedback about its content. He finalized and printed the text in 1837. The process undertaken for writing the Rule is one more example of Marcellin's spirit of collegiality and of his ability to listen to others and learn from them.

Marcellin's Rule for his brothers provided them with a framework for their religious life. In 1836, for example, the young men who formerly made vows privately, professed them in a public ceremony. Everyone, including superiors, were also required to do some manual work. The printed Rule of 1837 regularized many other aspects of the Little Brothers' lives.

Persecution increases

As 1831 dawned, the anti-clericals increased their attacks on the Church. The field of education was a convenient target. A royal ordinance called for the conscription for military service of all non-authorized teachers in religious schools. If this directive were implemented, the outcome would essentially cripple Marcellin's still unauthorized Institute.

Could the situation get any worse? Yes. New government officials of the Loire took specific aim at the Little Brothers. Scipion Mourgue, the new Prefect of the area, had this to say: "[The Marist Brothers Institute] is all the less worthy of encouragement in that it is publicly known that the subjects who come out of it are of a deplorable ignorance.... There [at Feurs] they brought what they call their teaching, which, I think, could be called the guarantee of ignorance on the cheap. Too long has France bowed down beneath the saber and the censer [that is, the king and the Church]."

Mourgue was further incensed when he discovered that the local people did not want to abandon the brothers' schools. So, he attacked them also. "I meet stupid local people," he said, "who want this degrading system maintained." Many of those "stupid local people," however, had already lived through the period of educational collapse after the Revolution of 1789; they had little interest in seeing history repeat itself.

School at Feurs is closed

Ignoring the people's wishes, the anti-clerical Mayor of the town of Feurs determined to drive the brothers out of their school there. He wrote Marcellin to say that the town could no longer afford the 1200 francs required to keep three brothers there. Marcellin replied that he was willing to accept 400 francs for the three and would make up the difference himself. The Mayor was not deterred; he ordered the brothers to leave.

Marcellin responded a second time with these words: "I note with resignation... the destruction of the establishment of the brothers, since I have made all efforts I ought to have made to save a school whose success was continually increasing. I am instructing them [the brothers] to give back the furniture that is the property of the town."

The founder's letter tells us a great deal about the man and his spirituality. In marked contrast to the earlier ranting of Scipion Mourgue, Marcellin expresses regret, resignation, and a sense of propriety — the brothers will return the furniture that belongs to the town. There are no threats, predictions of dire consequences, anger. The tone of serenity and inner peace, so obvious in Marcellin's words, suggests that the trials he faced throughout life purified his spirit.

Military conscription and the Brevet (a teaching certificate)

At that time military service in France often lasted from six to eight years. Teachers who were members of religious orders could be freed from this obligation only if their congregation had legal authority to conduct schools. Marcellin's Institute did not. He quickly turned his attention to solving this problem.

Marcellin had two alternatives available to keep his schools open. One, he could join his brothers with a legally-recognized congregation or, two, he could continue to pursue authorization for his Little Brothers. Officials of the Lyons Archdiocese counseled merger. The idea of a union with the brothers of Father Chaminade's Society of Mary, authorized in 1825, was given serious thought. Eventually, though, the Archdiocesan Council advised a merger with Father Querbes's Clerics of Saint Viateur.

Before the union could take place, Archbishop de Pins intervened. The Council had failed to obtain his approval for any merger prior to contacting Marcellin. De Pins encouraged the priest to try once again to gain independent legal authorization for his brothers. However, when it was not forthcoming, the Archbishop acquiesced to his Council's recommendation and advised the founder to join his brothers with Father Querbes's group.

Marcellin, however, feared such a merger would destroy the spirit among his Little Brothers. So, he continued to resist the calls for union.

Despite the lack of legal recognition and the pressure to merge his brothers with other groups, Marcellin continued to open schools. He was not lacking in invitations to do so. People in the country areas, suspicious of teachers graduating from the State Normal schools, pressed their elected officials to secure the services of the brothers. Even the passage of the Guizot Law, which invalidated virtually all the certificates that Marcellin's brothers had won, did not deter the founder.

The skies began to clear in January 1834. During supper one evening, Archbishop de Pins surprised Marcellin by saying, "I congratulate you on the course you took. I should be very sorry today if the proposal [for merger with the Clerics of Saint Viateur] had been carried out, for I see now that I was misinformed concerning your Society."

Unfortunately, government approbation for his Institute would elude Marcellin throughout his life. Events in French history at that time worked against his petition. The Law of Associations, passed in February 1834 and meant to curb working class militancy, was used to delay authorization. While a roadblock for the founder, this government legislation was unable to prevent a violent uprising that took place in Lyons in April 1834.

Marist priests win approval

Earlier in our story we met Vicar General Bochard and learned what a cross he was to Marcellin. He was also a cross to Jean-Claude Colin and his fellow Marist priests at Belley. Bochard was competitive, but did not like competition. Consequently, he opposed Church authorization of any congregation whose ends resembled those of his Society of the Cross of Jesus. Unfortunately, the apostolate the young Marist priests had in mind was similar to that of Bochard's group.

Father Courveille proved to be another roadblock to authorization. We have already seen that the man lacked judgment and a spirit of discernment. He was also deficient in the skills needed to get the group organized. Father Colin eventually took on that task.

The bishops of the region initially proved to be still another obstacle to the young Marist priests and their dream of Church approval. What bishop is going to say "yes" to a congregation whose existence will reduce the number of priests in his charge?

Despite these difficulties, by 1825 the Marist priests received permission to live in two communities, one in Belley and the other at the Hermitage. Father Colin was named superior for the first, Marcellin for the second. The latter, although briefly disheartened, was devoted to the group of Marist priests and worked hard to see that they were established. He confided to one of his brothers, "To my mind the work of the [Marist] priests appears to be also of such importance that, were it necessary for its success, I would be prepared to sacrifice all that I have."

Over time, the two dioceses, Lyons and Belley, permitted the priests to cross diocesan boundaries in their work. Permission was also eventually given for a third community to be established in Valbenoîte. Father Séon, who years earlier had confided to Marcellin his hope that the congregation of Marist priests would be established and that he could be a member, was named superior.

Marcellin worked to build up other branches of the Society of Mary. In August 1832 he encouraged three young women to join Jean-Marie Chavoin's Marist Sisters at Bon-Repos, in Belley. He eventually directed no fewer than fifteen candidates toward that group of women religious. One was his niece, another the sister of one of the brothers. His enthusiasm high and his heart hopeful, Marcellin must have thought that formal Church approval for the Marist dream would be realized shortly. An August 1833 trip to Rome by Father Colin quickly brought him back to reality.

Colin goes to Rome

Jean-Claude Colin, determined to gain approbation for the Marist group, traveled to Rome in the summer of 1833. There he met with frustration. First, he had difficulty obtaining an audience with the Pope. Next, he found that a Society that included priests, sisters, brothers, and a Third Order was greeted with suspicion by Vatican authorities. They saw it as a huge group dominated by the French. Gallicanism still struck fear in the hearts of Roman Church authorities.

In December of the same year, however, Colin received from Cardinal Odescalchi, Prefect of the Vatican Congregation of Bishops and Regulars, general approval for the idea of the Marist group. The Cardinal did suggest that the enterprise was too big. He also handed the matter over to Cardinal Castracane for further study. The latter quickly came to this conclusion: "This Society made up of four branches was considered... to be a delirium. Approval of this monstrous organization was not possible."

In April of 1834 Cardinal Odescalchi wrote to the Ordinaries of both Lyons and Belley to inform them that Rome found unacceptable the plans for Colin's Society of Mary. He cited several reasons. One, there was no need for the Marist Brothers since the De La Salle group existed already and apparently had the same goal. Two, so many congregations of women religious existed in France already that it was almost impossible to count them; why add another? Three, the proposed Third Order of laity was judged to be an "outlandish" idea, setting aside the bishop's power in favor of the Superior General of the Marist Society. Was there any good news in this litany of woe? Yes: Rome supported Colin's request to form a new clerical congregation and to have a Superior General elected for it.

Despite his disappointment with the Vatican's decision about the four-branched Marist Society, Marcellin quickly offered the Marist Fathers of Valbenoîte a large property at Izieux, not far from the Hermitage. It was known as La Grange-Payre and had come to the priest through a benefactor. A secluded place, it was ideal for recollection. Marcellin wanted to be sure that members of the Marist Fathers did not lose their religious spirit by becoming too busy. He was also concerned that this new Marist group led by Séon at Valbenoîte have a place to form new members.

Colin eventually decided not to take the property. But Marcellin helped in other ways, for example, assisting Colin in the formation of the Brothers of Saint Joseph, a group of lay brothers in the society of Marist priests.

Opportunity knocks

Early in 1835 Vatican authorities informed the bishops of Lyons and Belley that the Marist priests could, on application to Rome, become an interdiocesan congregation and elect a Superior General. No specific work was assigned to the group.

Full recognition as an apostolic Institute was not long in coming. The Vatican was disappointed by the lack of response to its appeal for missionaries to go to Oceania. Vicar General Cholleton heard that Rome was looking for a congregation to fill the gap. He passed along the news to Pompallier, a priest who had served as a chaplain at the Hermitage, who quickly informed Colin. The young Marist priests seized the opportunity presented to them and took the mission of Oceania as their work. On April 29th, 1836, the long awaited approval for the new Institute of priests arrived from Rome.

With his efforts to win approbation now having born fruit, Colin wanted to step aside and let Vicar General Cholleton, an aspiring Marist, take on leadership for the group. A second message from Rome, however, caused him to change his mind. The work of the Marist priests was not to be restricted to the mission of Oceania; they could also set up an apostolate in France.

While Colin did not fancy being the superior of a group whose sole work was in overseas missions, he thought he could direct a group with this wider scope for its work. He agreed to stay on, at least until the election of a superior for the new Society. The voting took place in September 1836. The result? Colin was the group's choice. He won all the votes except one, his own.

Marcellin was delighted with Rome's approval of the Society of priests. Its members were always close to his heart. Their affection and esteem for him were also obvious. In 1839 the group elected him as one of the Assistants General to Father Colin.

His delight was only augmented by the decision to take Oceania as a mission for the group. The founder had always hoped to serve overseas; his name, in fact, headed the list of Marists volunteering for the Pacific. Unfortunately, age and health had become obstacles. Also, his continuing presence as leader of the brothers was critical at this time and for the foreseeable future. He supported the missions by sending a small group of brothers along with the first Marist priests who traveled to the Pacific.

Pompallier was named Vicar Apostolic for the Missions of Oceania and shortly thereafter was ordained a bishop at the Church of the Immaculate Conception in Rome. He and his group of four priests and three brothers went to Fourvière and placed their missionary work under Mary's protection. They then traveled to Paris, and on Christmas Eve 1836 departed for the Pacific from the port of Le Havre. Speaking of the brothers, Marcellin had once said, "A brother is a man for whom the world is not large enough." The ship's departure from port, with his three brothers on board, was the first step he took in making that vision a reality.

Reflection questions

Sometimes setbacks in life can turn out to be great sources of personal and spiritual growth. Identify a setback in your own life; in what ways did it challenge you to grow more as a person and as a disciple of Jesus?

The founder was delighted with the approval of the Society of Marist priests. For what events or decisions in your own life do you give thanks to God?

Chapter VII

A Man and a Saint for All Seasons, and for All Times...

$\mathcal{W}$e are near our story's end. Until his death Marcellin continued to pursue authorization for his Little Brothers, traveling to Paris and doing battle with one or another government official or agency. At times, those with power to give approval agreed to do so if he made concessions: restrict his brothers' schools, for example, to certain geographic areas, or confine them to towns of 1000 people or less. The founder was unwilling to be hemmed in. Eventually his work for official government recognition came to naught.

Authorization did come with time in 1842, two years after Marcellin's death, when Father Mazelier's Brothers of Christian Instruction of the Diocese of Valence merged with the Little Brothers. The former held legal status in three Departments. While not all that the founder had hoped for, it was a beginning.

The Institute continued to grow but Marcellin was careful not to overburden the brothers or to stretch his resources too thin. In 1837, for example, Father Fontbonne, once a chaplain at the Hermitage and now a missionary in Saint Louis, Missouri, wrote requesting brothers to help with the work in America. Marcellin responded, "All the brothers were jealous of the two who had been chosen to go to Polynesia.... I would be happy to send you brothers to help in the work in America, if it were at all possible." Oceania, however, remained the sole overseas mission for a number of years.

Marcellin continued to marvel at the growth of the Marist group in general. He once said to his fellow priests, "We who are at the commencement of our work are but raw stones thrown into the foundation. One does not use polished stones for that. There is something marvelous in the commencement of our Society. What is marvelous is that God has wished such people to accomplish his work."

Marcellin falls ill

In the course of 1839 the founder fell ill. Since his sickness of 1825, he suffered constant pain in his side. Later he developed an inflammation of the stomach and vomited frequently. On his return from Paris in 1838, Brother Jean-Baptiste remarked, "It was easy to see that his end was fast approaching."

Concerned about Marcellin's deteriorating condition, Father Colin, Superior General of the Marists, arranged for an election to choose the founder's successor. Brother François, who as a ten year-old boy had been brought by his brother to one of Marcellin's catechism lessons, was elected overwhelmingly. Brothers Louis-Marie and Jean-Baptiste were chosen as his assistants.

On Ash Wednesday 1840 Marcellin was seized by sharp back pain; it remained with him until his death three months later. Despite his deteriorating physical condition, he refused to stay in bed, and instead attended community activities, so as to be with his brothers. They, in turn, arranged for a doctor to be available. Marcellin made a will on March 22nd; he left all that he owned to the Institute at the Hermitage.

On Holy Thursday the founder made his way to La Grange-Payre to celebrate Mass. This property, once offered to Father

Colin and the Marist Fathers, was now the site of a school and a house of formation. When the brothers protested that he lacked the strength for this journey, Marcellin said, "Let me go, for this is the last visit I shall be able to pay to those good brothers and their children."

Over the next few weeks, the founder became progressively more incapacitated, and after May 3rd was no longer able to celebrate Mass for the brothers. With his sufferings increasing by the day, he sensed eventually that he had little time left. He asked Brother Stanislaus to assemble all the brothers in the community room so that he could address them for the last time.

"Remember that you are brothers," he told them, "and that Mary is your common Mother. Bear with one another and do not forget that it is the practice of charity that will make of your religious life a life of sweetness. Love your vocation, persevere in it, it is the means that God has chosen for your salvation." His voice growing ever weaker, he concluded with these words, "I cannot say anymore, I will conclude by asking pardon... for all the bad example I have given you." The young men were choked with emotion. Falling to their knees, many began to sob, so deep was their love for this priest who had been a father and older brother to them. Capturing that love in words, Father Bélier, a missionary priest present when Marcellin died, said, "Never was there a prince of this world surrounded with such tender care in his last moments."

The end

Death came for Marcellin Champagnat early on a Saturday morning. The date: June 6th, 1840. The brothers had kept vigil all night; he slipped away as they recited community prayers at daybreak.

Two days later, the founder's body was laid to rest in the Hermitage's cemetery, not far from the site of the tiny Chapel in the Woods. His Spiritual Testament, not written in his hand but expressing the sentiments of his heart, had been read three weeks before, on May 18th. He asked for pardon from all whom he might have offended, expressed allegiance to the Superior of the Marist Fathers, and gave thanks for being able to die as a member of the Society of Mary. Then, he turned his attention to his brothers.

There was nothing petty about Marcellin Champagnat. It is not surprising, therefore, that obedience and love were the two virtues he recommended to his early followers. They are, after all, the foundation of community. Obedience is its mainstay; love binds all other virtues together and makes them perfect. Of this second, there was to be no limit. Marcellin loved his brothers; he expected no less from them, each one for the other.

Throughout his life as a priest, the founder was fond of saying, "To rear children properly, we must love them, and love them all equally." The virtue of love, therefore, was to be not only the foundation of community but also of a distinctive Marist method of evangelization and education. It had been Mary's way with Jesus; it was now to be the way of all who followed the dream that so captured the heart of this country priest and his early brothers.

Marcellin warned his followers against rivalry with other congregations and completed his testament with a summary of the spirituality of his Little Brothers. "Practice the presence of God," he told them. "It is the soul of prayer, meditation, and all the virtues. Let humility and simplicity be the characteristics that distinguish you from others, and maintain always a spirit of poverty and detachment. Have a filial and tender devotion to Mary, he counseled, make her loved in every place. Love and be faithful to your vocation, and persevere in it courageously."

The world into which Marcellin Champagnat was born in 1789 was beginning to convulse with the tremors of change. The one he left fifty-one years later had seen war and peace, prosperity and hardship, the death of one understanding of Church and the birth of another. A man of his times, he carried within himself all the greatness and limitations of the people of his age. Suffering tempered him, setbacks strengthened him, determination drove him, and grace helped him move beyond his circumstances.

Marcellin Champagnat, priest of the Society of Mary, Superior and Founder of the Little Brothers of Mary. An apostle to youth and an example of practical Christianity. He was a man and saint for his season and time; he is both for ours also.

Reflection questions

The lives of saints make the gospel message more evident for us. In what way does Marcellin's life help you understand and live out the gospel more fully?

In his Spiritual Testament, the founder expresses joy at being able to die as a member of the Society of Mary. Looking ahead to the end of your own life, for what response to God's love would you want to be able to give thanks?

Afterword

$\mathscr{A}$t our story's outset we asked this question, "Who was Marcellin Champagnat?" Here at its end, we have our answer: the future saint was a man of God, a man of his times, and a man of passion and practicality, and not without his flaws.

A man of God

Not born a saint, Marcellin Champagnat spent a lifetime becoming one. The founder gave his early brothers this sound advice: "To become a brother," he said, "is to undertake to become a saint." He came to this awareness through the hard lessons of his own life.

As we have seen, Marcellin's mother, Marie Thérèse, and aunt, Louise, were the first to awaken a spiritual life in the young boy. Their example and direction were foundational. He absorbed from both women practices of piety and the spiritual heritage of the high plateau region.

The founder was fortunate to grow up in the district of Marlhes. A region of deep faith, it claimed Saint John Francis Regis as its patron and made his shrine a place of pilgrimage. This saint impressed young Marcellin, and influenced his spiritual formation.

We know also that the founder had great devotion to Mary,

the mother of Jesus. He lived in the Marial district of bishops Pothin and Irenaeus, and in a country influenced by the writings of Mariologists such as Olier and Grignon de Montfort. The future saint's devotion to the Mother of God was shaped initially by the religious practice and theology of late eighteenth and early nineteenth-century France.

Jesus, though, and not Mary, was the destination of Marcellin's journey of faith. The mystery of the Incarnation was at the heart of his spirituality. The founder's Christology emphasized Jesus in his human nature. While his own writings are not the source of the brothers' attachment to Christ through Crib, Cross, and Altar, he approved of this practice, and encouraged his followers to use these havens for reflection and prayer.

Growing in a life of faith

An ongoing process of conversion marked Marcellin's ever deepening relationship with God. In his spiritual quest as a young man, the founder first gave emphasis to self-discipline, achieving it only with the help of a well thought-out program of prayer and penance during seminary holidays and as a young priest in La Valla.

Next, he relied on the rule of law. It gave him a guide for living, and helped him control his behavior and achieve a certain serenity of soul. Thankfully, though, Marcellin's common sense and good judgment aided him in rising above the legalism and rigidity that characterized so much of the moral theology taught in early nineteenth-century French seminaries.

Eventually, the founder arrived at a point where he built his spirituality upon the foundation of love of God and other people. As mentioned earlier, Marcellin loved the Lord with His very human nature. Gregarious, he also loved people and enjoyed spending time with them. The future saint understood that one way to a loving relationship with God was through loving relationships with others. In time, he came to realize that each person he met was an image of the risen Savior whom he had come to know and love so well.

We know already that three elements lay at the heart of the spirituality Marcellin passed on to his Little Brothers: confidence in God's presence, devotion to Mary and reliance on her protection, and the practice of the uncomplicated virtues of simplicity and humility. The founder's spirituality was incarnational and decidedly Marial.

An incarnational spirituality

The first evident aspect of Marcellin's spirituality was its incarnational nature. This element was the source of his practice of the presence of God. He believed that Jesus was close at hand. Consequently, his conversations with the Lord continued uninterrupted, and his confidence in Jesus and abandonment to His will grew over time. The future saint often quoted the words of Psalm 127, "If the Lord does not build a house, in vain do its builders toil."

Marcellin's incarnational spirituality is also apparent in the wording of many of his letters. In an April 8th, 1839 note to Brother Marie-Laurent, for example, the founder wrote: "Your letter, my very dear friend, greatly aroused my compassion. Since then I never approach the holy altar without recommending you to Him in whom we never hope in vain, who can help us overcome the greatest obstacles." The future saint signed his letters with this characteristic phrase, "I leave you in the pure hearts of Jesus and Mary," and was fond of saying, "These are such good places; it is so good to be there."

The place of Mary

A second feature of Marcellin's spirituality was its Marial dimension. The founder was strongly attached to Mary. He named his brothers after her; she became a central part of their spiritual heritage; he saw her as the Institute's first Superior.

The future saint's relationship with the Mother of Jesus matured over time. He had complete trust in her and confidence in her protection, saying often to his brothers, "With Mary, we have everything; without her, we are nothing; because Mary has her adorable son, either in her arms or in her heart." His dealings with Mary show not the slightest trace of embarrassment. The closer he feels to her, the more she is present to him as a living person. Eventually a relationship between two people constituted his devotion to her; she became his confidant. He often used the familiar form of the French expression, "you know," in his Marial prayer, revealing a relationship of some intimacy.

Marcellin's devotion to Mary was expressed externally in sermons, novenas, and letters. His February 4th, 1831 letter to Brothers Antoine and Gonzaga is but one example of this aspect of his spiritual life. The founder wrote, "Get Mary on your side; tell her that after you have done all you can, it's just too bad for her if her affairs don't go well." Marcellin trusted completely in Mary's intercession: once her petitioners had done their best, she had to take responsibility for seeing them through.

The founder encouraged his brothers to follow his lead in their devotion to Mary. For example, he asked them to display a picture or statue of her in the house, and wanted them to carry on their person something to remind them of her. Later, he advised the touching practices of offering to Mary the keys of the house, and of placing the names of brothers not resident in the Hermitage community in a heart hung around the neck of the statue he referred to as "Our Lady of the Hermitage." "She is in charge of us," he said. "She is our patroness, our protectress."

Marcellin also counseled his brothers to take Mary as their Mother. She was to be a model for imitation, and a person to be approached with childlike confidence. At the Annunciation, Mary's response to God was trusting and direct. The founder wanted his brothers to be no less wholehearted in their "Yes." In the Rule of 1837, the future saint included a special prayer, "Abandonment to the Most Holy Mother of God."

What does the founder's devotion to Mary tell us about his personality? A great deal. Marcellin was a man who, over time, became increasingly more aware of his limitations. He realized that the gifts required for the adventure in which he found himself exceeded his natural capacities. How explain its success? Sincere of conscience, the future saint gave credit for all that had been accomplished to Mary, whose help he had always requested and whose inspiration he had followed as faithfully as possible.

The uncomplicated virtues of simplicity and humility

The practice of the uncomplicated virtues of simplicity and humility was the third essential element of the founder's spirituality. Simplicity was the quality that characterized Marcellin Champagnat. He was direct, enthusiastic, confident. He encouraged his brothers to develop the same traits.

The future saint was also humble: as he grew to maturity, he came to know and accept himself. Marcellin was not a man of pretense. Similarly, he challenged his brothers to be sincere and unpretentious.

A man of his times

The Church of early nineteenth-century France faced a crisis of innovation. The world in which it found itself had changed quickly and decisively; the Church's response to this shakeup had to be inventive and resourceful. Sad to say, once the dust settled, many clergy looked for ways to re-establish the past. The future would not belong to them. Rather, people like Marcellin Champagnat would shape it. Not an intellectual in the academic sense, Marcellin showed that his abilities lay in his capacity for coping with the practical details of life, and the concrete realities of human relationships.

The eyes of faith might conclude that God's humor played a role in having a man who was not a scholar, and who made errors in his use of written French, as the founder of a teaching Institute. The future saint, though, saw an urgent need to evangelize poor young people, and responded with a simple pedagogy: love children, especially those most in need, lead them to the Lord, form them to be good Christians and citizens. In January 1836, he wrote his brothers: "I desire and wish that, following the example of Jesus, you have a tender love for children. With holy zeal break for them the spiritual bread of religion."

The founder had a buoyant, enthusiastic approach to education. What characteristics distinguished his Marist pedagogy from that of others? Simple presence among the young, collaboration with parents, a spirit of family, a central place for Mary, love of work, a special concern for the most neglected.

When it came to educational techniques, Marcellin was not an original thinker. He sought advice and borrowed what looked most effective. The De La Salle Brothers, for example, were respected Christian educators in the days prior to and following the Revolution of 1789. While the characteristic spirits of the two congregations differ, Marcellin was not reluctant to use those of their methods and practices that would be a help to his brothers.

And help they needed! The founder's early recruits often lacked basic education, having been formed more by poverty and hard work than by books. As we have seen, he labored tirelessly to train them in both catechetics and secular subjects.

A man of passion and practicality, and not without his faults

What heritage did Marcellin Champagnat pass along to his brothers? Surely not a library of theological and religious reflections. Rather, his legacy consisted of a generous heart, a passion for the Gospel of Jesus Christ, and a common sense and practical approach to life. Simply put, the founder was a man of passion and of action.

The Hermitage, built by the future saint and his early brothers, tells us something about the passionate character of the man. The building, constructed by using roughly-fashioned stones, projects these qualities: strength, determination, endurance. Its setting amidst gardens, meadows, clear streams, and the region's seasonal changes suggests still other aspects of the founder's personality: a love of life, compassion, and understanding. A fire burned bright in Marcellin's spirit. His welcome was always warm; he was a man of heart and affection.

Undoubtedly, it was his passion that made the founder such a charismatic person, not only to the young people whom he attracted with such ease, but also to all whose lives he touched.

A practical man of action

Marcellin Champagnat had a practical mind. This trait was evident throughout his life. He paid for his early seminary formation using money earned from his successful business raising and selling sheep. Later, after he had established his Little Brothers, the founder insisted that a garden be part of each house in which they would live. Marcellin was convinced that tending a vegetable garden would build a sense of family spirit, and keep the brothers in touch with the lives of those whom they were called to serve. By providing their own vegetables, they would also minimize the cost to the parish and town for their support.

The founder's strong will made him a determined and persistent leader. These qualities were great gifts. No doubt, at times, they could also be maddening. Like all of us, the future saint had those areas in his life where he fell short of the ideal. He is a saint, not by his own merit, but rather because he allowed God's grace into his heart, where it took root and flourished. He suggested as much, when he wrote in his Spiritual Testament: "There are difficulties in living the life of a good religious, but grace makes all things easy."

Marcellin Champagnat took seriously the Good News of Jesus Christ. He was a holy man because he lived his ordinary life exceptionally well, and did ordinary things with extraordinary love. Having discovered the joy of the Gospel and letting it transform him, the founder wanted to share with others, particularly the young, all that he had seen and heard. "To love God," Marcellin often said, "to love God and to labor to make God known and loved, this is what a brother's life should be." With these few words, the future saint painted his own portrait and recounted his own story. His was a heart that knew no bounds.

References

Avit FMS, Frère. *Abrégé des Annales de Frère Avit*. (Roma: Tipografia S. Pio X, 1972)

Farrell FMS, Brother Stephen. *Achievement from the Depths*. (Drummoyne, NSW: Marist Brothers, 1984).

Gibson FMS, Brother Romuald. *Father Champagnat: The Man and his Spirituality*. (Rome: Fratelli Maristi, 1971).

Furet, Frère Jean-Baptiste. *Vie de Joseph-Benoît-Marcellin Champagnat*. (Lyons: Frères Maristes, 1956).

Lanfrey, FMS, Frère André. *Marcellin Champagnat and Les Frères Maristes: Instituteurs congrégationistes au XIXe siècle*. (Paris: Éditions Don Bosco, 1999).

Masson, Robert. *Marcellin Champagnat: Les Improbables de Dieu*. (Saint-Maur: Parole et Silence, 1999).

McMahon, FMS, Brother Frederick. *Strong Mind, Gentle Heart*. (Drummoyne, NSW: Marist Brothers, 1988).

Sester, FMS, Brother Paul (Ed.). *Letters of Marcellin J.B. Champagnat 1789-1840* (Trans. Brother Leonard Voegtle, FMS). (Rome: Casa Generalizia Dei Fratelli Maristi, 1991).

Sester, FMS, Brother Paul. *Mary in the Life of Marcellin Champagnat*, Marist Notebooks, no. 8, January 1996, pp. 29-38.

Zind, FMS, Frère Pierre. *Bx. M. Champagnat: son oeuvre scolaire dans son contexte historique*. (Rome: Maison Generale des Frères Maristes, 1991).

VOCATION INFORMATION

Today 5000 Marist Brothers are evangelizing young people in 74 countries throughout the world. If you believe that God is calling you to serve with them, and would like more information about the Little Brothers of Mary, their life together and their mission, please contact the brothers in your country or in one close to it, as listed below. For a listing of all countries in which the brothers minister, write to: Fratelli Maristi, Piazzale M. Champagnat, 2, CP 10.250, 00144, Roma, Italia, call: (39)06-545-171, or e-mail: fms@rm.nettuno.it.

Vocation Promoter
80 Nicholson Street
Fitzroy
Vic 3065
Australia

Vocation Promoter
8 Mills Street 2141
P.O. Box 254
Lidcombe NSW 1825
Australia

Vocation Promoter
Tatum
P. B. M. 46 BAMENDA
N. W. Province
Republic of Cameroon

Vocation Promoter
Marist Brothers
Suva Street
P.O. Box 86
SUVA
Fiji

Vocation Promoter
Champagnat House
P. O. Box 8583
Kumasi
Ghana

Vocation Promoter
Marist House
10 Partickhill Road
GLASGOW, G11 5BL
Great Britain

Vocation Promoter
Marist Brothers
Maria Shanti Illam
Mela Street
Uyyakkondan Thirumalai
Trichy 620 102
India

Vocation Promoter
Moyle Park College
Clondalkin
DUBLIN 22
Ireland

Vocation Promoter
Marist Brothers
P. O. Box 160
Sori Karungu
South-Nyanza
Kenya

Vocation Promoter
Marist Brothers
Bikenibeu
Tarawa
Kiribati, Central Pacific
Kiribati

Vocation Promoter
Marist Brothers
85-1 Hapchong-dong, Mapo-gu
Seoul-shi 121-200
C.P.O. Box 5636
Seoul, 100-656
South Korea

Vocation Promoter
Champagnat House
P. O. Box 46
Malirana, Dezda
Malawi

Vocation Promoter
1A, Jalan 10/3
46000 PETALING JAYA
Selangor
Malaysia

Vocation Promoter
Marist Brothers
P.O. Box 24400, Royal Oak
Auckland 3k
New Zealand

Vocation Promoter
P.O. Box 307
Orlu
Imo State
Nigeria

Vocation Promoter
Sargodha Catholic School
P. O. Box 110
CHAK 47 N.B.
SARGODHA
Pakistan

Vocation Promoter
Marist Brothers
P. O. Box 107
Wewak E.S.P. 531
Papua New Guinea

Vocation Promoter
P. O. Box 42
9500 General Santos City
Philippines

Vocation Promoter
Mulivai School
P. O. Box 4
Apia
Western Samoa

Vocation Promoter
Champagnat House
15, Flower Road
SINGAPORE 549404
Singapore

Vocation Promoter
Laumanasa House
P. O. Box 82
Honiara
Solomon Islands

Vocation Promoter
Marist Brothers
P. O. Box 1945
Uitenhage
6230 South Africa

Vocation Promoter
Paul Ambrose Niwasa
105/2, Agaradaguru Mawata
Tudella, JA-ELA
Sri Lanka

Vocation Promoter
Marist Brothers
P.O. Box 10554
Pamba Road
MWANZA
Tanzania, East Africa

Vocation Promoter
Marist Brothers
Takuilau College, Lapaha
P.O. Box 822
Nuku'alofa
Tonga

Vocation Promoter
Marist Brothers
101-40 92nd Street
Ozone Park, NY 11416
USA

Vocation Promoter
Saint Anne Residence
10114 South Leavitt
Chicago, IL 60643
USA

Vocation Promoter
Marist Brothers
P. O. Box 80663
Kabwe
Zambia

Vocation Promoter
Marist Brothers
6 Belfast Road
P.O. Avondale
Harare
Zimbabwe

This book was designed and published by St. Pauls/
Alba House, the publishing arm of the Society of
St. Paul, an international religious congregation of
priests and brothers dedicated to serving the Church
through the communications media. For information regarding this and associated ministries of the
Pauline Family of Congregations, write to the Vocation Director, Society of St. Paul, 7050 Pinehurst,
Dearborn, Michigan 48126 or check our internet site,
www.albahouse.org